EDIT IS A FOUR-LE ___ ___ ᴡ UꞪᴅ

Don't know how to edit your work? Not sure when it's ready to send out? Glynis Scrivens' book answers all your questions. Follow the excellent advice given by Glynis and the experienced contributors she has included and reap the rewards. If you are serious about sending out your best possible work you cannot be without *Edit is a Four Letter Word*.
Lynne Hackles

Edit is a Four Letter Word will show you how to fine-tune your editing procedure. A writer's editing process is as personal as their writing style, but it's always useful to know how others do it. As the book says, there is no obvious cut-off point. Knowing when to stop is just as important as knowing what to edit. Even amongst these pages, writers disagree. (Should you have your spellchecker switched on, or off?) But that's not the point. Glynis has written a book that shares the tips and methods other writers use, enabling you to select, refine, hone and perfect your own editing technique. There's no right or wrong way to edit: just your way. This book will help you discover your way of editing.
Simon Whaley

Whatever you write, a properly edited manuscript can make the world of difference when submitting your work. This book, packed with hints and tips and the experiences of published writers is all you need when setting about the daunting task of editing. Glynis guides you through the process from beginning to end in a friendly and easy to read format. A must for any writer's bookshelf.
Teresa Ashby

Edit is a Four-Letter Word

How to Create the Best First Impression

Edit is a
Four-Letter Word

How to Create the Best First Impression

Glynis Scrivens

**COMPASS
BOOKS**

Winchester, UK
Washington, USA

First published by Compass Books, 2015
Compass Books is an imprint of John Hunt Publishing Ltd., Laurel House, Station Approach,
Alresford, Hants, SO24 9JH, UK
office1@jhpbooks.net
www.johnhuntpublishing.com
www.compass-books.net

For distributor details and how to order please visit the 'Ordering' section on our website.

Text copyright: Glynis Scrivens 2014

ISBN: 978 1 78279 522 3
Library of Congress Control Number: 2015937443

A CIP catalogue record for this book is available from the British Library.

Design: Lee Nash

Printed in the USA by Edwards Brothers Malloy

We operate a distinctive and ethical publishing philosophy in all
areas of our business, from our global network of authors to
production and worldwide distribution.

CONTENTS

This book is dedicated to my mother, Elsie, who instilled in us the importance of good grammar. If our home had ever caught fire, she'd have grabbed her treasured copy of Fowler's *Modern English Usage.*
And to my father, Raymond, who taught us "if a job is worth doing, it's worth doing properly".

Acknowledgements

In putting together this book, I've asked around 20 writers how they edit. Their honest responses shed light on the editing process, and the many individual ways of achieving the same result: a polished final draft. I also interviewed editors, competition judges and a literary agent. I'd like to thank each and every one for sharing their thoughts and methods: Teresa Ashby, Greg Barron, Tim Bowler, Hope Clark, Dani Collins, Christopher Currie, Sarah Duncan, Sarah England, Jill Finlay, John Floyd, Della Galton, Rachelle Gardner, Lynne Hackles, Deborah Halverson, Samantha Hazell, Peter Lovesey, Monica McInerney, Rebecca LuElla Miller, Phil Murphy, Sheila O'Flanagan, Iain Pattison, Liz Smith, Ginny Swart, Bruce Thomson, Jane Wenham-Jones, Simon Whaley and Kate Willoughby.

Special thanks to writing buddy Lynne Hackles for reading my draft and showing how an unwieldy 4800 word chapter could be split into two smaller ones of a more respectable length.

Thanks for Rachelle Gardner for permission to quote from her blog.

And thanks to my husband Denzil for proofreading the final version.

The seeds of this book were sown in my articles for *Writers' Forum*. Thank you, Carl Styants, for your support and encouragement.

And thanks to Suzanne Ruthven of Compass Books for supporting this project.

Introduction

Editing is all about creating a good first impression. And you need to know exactly who it is you're hoping to impress.

There's an ad where a group of young men sits outside an interview room. In their dark suits, white shirts and ties, they look indistinguishable from each other.

Just like your story or novel sitting in an editor's slush pile. Smartened up and polished since the first draft, but rubbing shoulders with hundreds of other smartened up manuscripts. Only one will be chosen.

How do you shorten the odds in your favour?

In the ad, one young man notices portraits of the company directors on the wall. He slips outside and shaves his head.

When the interviewer emerges, he's bald. The camera shifts to the portraits. Every director of this company is bald.

Guess which candidate has positioned himself to be accepted?

That's exactly the kind of advantage you give your work when you edit it to fit the specific requirements of a publisher.

Make it look as if it already belongs there.

There's no one quick way to do this.

A piece of writing needs to be edited at several different levels. It's a big job, best done by reducing it to a number of clearly defined stages, so nothing important is forgotten.

Think about those young men. They've studied for the interview. On the day they've showered, ironed their shirts, combed their hair, and shaved. Some will have asked for a second opinion. "Should I wear a black suit? Which tie should I wear?"

The wife of one may have cleaned away a smear of toothpaste from his moustache. It's not always possible to notice every detail ourselves.

A second opinion can save embarrassment and immediate rejection.

The company may have provided a list of common mistakes to avoid, perhaps on their website. If the criteria state "all applicants require a masters degree in industrial relations", they expect this requirement to be met.

Just as publishers expect writers to strictly adhere to the guidelines they provide.

Again, it's unusual to get the first job we apply for. Often it takes several interviews.

Each needs to be prepared for on an individual basis.

Similarly your manuscript needs to be carefully edited for each publication you submit it to until it finds a home.

Every marketplace has its own individual house style. Some magazines use double inverted commas for dialogue, others use single. Magazines have clearly defined pages allocated for fiction and specific word counts. Publishers require novels of a particular genre and length. These requirements change with new editors, when one company takes over another, or in response to reader demand. Writing for today's markets requires ongoing research and the flexibility to adapt to new demands.

This book will show you ways to smarten up your story or novel. There's a checklist to use, and examples to study. Emphasis is placed on the editing process, by following the experiences of novelists, short story writers, editors and competition judges. Study their advice and apply it to your own work.

You learn to write by writing. And you learn to edit by editing. There are how-to books covering every aspect of writing – characters, dialogue, plot, viewpoint and so on. That material can't be covered in a book of this nature. What is presented here is the process of editing. And we have much to gain by seeing how other writers go about editing their work. There's no shortage of books about the specifics of grammar and punctuation. But there's more to good editing than mastering these.

And there's no one correct way to edit.

Writers need to evolve their own system of editing.

What helps one might get in the way for another.

In writing this book, I've interviewed a range of writers willing to share their editing experiences. Some like Peter Lovesey and Sheila O'Flanagan are well known and successful. Others like Greg Barron are relative newcomers. Each shares the nitty-gritty of how they go about this task.

Their approaches differ widely.

Take what you need from each, and continue on your own journey. Editing is how you make your story truly shine. Rough diamonds are lovely but to become dazzling, they need to be cut and polished.

Edit is a four-letter word. It requires other four-letter words. Work. Task. Slog. Time.

If you want to be the smart candidate who shaved his head, read on.

Part I

The Nature of Editing

When NOT to Edit

Get that first draft written

Editing starts when writing is finished. Most writers find the best approach is to tie and gag their internal editor while writing that first draft. We can be writing a sentence and grind to a halt, an insistent voice in our head saying, "Stop, this is rubbish. You can do better."

You probably can do better. That's the purpose of editing. Fixing up what you've written so that it gleams.

But wait until you've finished that first draft.

For every writer who does finish, there are dozens of others who never make it to the end. Why? They convince themselves it's not good enough.

So, odd as it seems, this book on editing starts by outlining when NOT to edit. Otherwise you might end up as one of those dozens. Someone else with a half-finished manuscript.

It doesn't matter what you're writing, the principle's the same. Learn to shut out that voice in your head and just get on with it. Allow yourself to complete what Anne Lamott so wisely describes as a shitty first draft. Her book *Bird by Bird* should be handy whenever you're tackling a writing project. She gives you permission to get it down rather than to get it right.

My first drafts certainly fit Anne Lamott's description of shitty. That doesn't mean they won't be published. Some of my shitty first drafts have eventually sold to six different publications. Yours could too.

How do I silence my inner critic? Writing everything down by hand works for me. If I sit at the computer, I have higher expectations of that first draft. Something inside me freezes. Gets performance anxiety. For some reason, scribbling in margins, writing wherever, works for me. The messier the first draft, the less likely I am to fumble and come to a standstill. And when I get to the end of a page, it's satisfying to turn over to the next one. The physical thing shows you're making progress. Something you can't experience with a computer screen.

And why stay indoors if it's a lovely day? You might be surprised to know I'm drafting this while sitting on the sand at Coolum beach. I'm using the back of some old envelopes I found in my handbag. How could that be scary? And because it isn't, the words are flowing. If I was sitting at a desk, looking at a blank screen, I'd feel that I needed something important to write. And then I'd feel I wasn't in the right mood, or any of a dozen other ways of feeling inadequate to the task. Nobody feels inadequate listening to the ocean, watching seagulls, and scribbling as the fancy takes them.

Writing by hand might work for you too. Why not try it?

Eight different writers = Eight different writing experiences

It always helps to listen to other writers telling how they work. To find out where they struggle and what they find useful. I asked eight writers how they silence their inner critic when they're writing a first draft. I got eight different answers. See if any of their experiences tally with your own. Is there something here you can apply to your own writing?

Iain Pattison

Short story expert, competition judge and creative writing tutor Iain Pattison keeps his inner critic well and truly silenced.

"Everyone has an internal editor but I keep mine tied up and gagged in a box until the first draft of my story is finished. I can't think of anything worse than having a heckler in my head making me question what I'm creating.

"An internal editor – or critic – is just your own insecurities speaking, like a gleefully malicious back seat driver. Give it a chance and it'll make you crash. The trick is never stop in the middle of writing to reread the work or tweak it. Don't give the inner editor an opportunity to start whispering. Keep pushing on, weaving the magic spell. Get to your destination. There's plenty of time later to stick on your critic's hat and put what you've produced under intense scrutiny.

"Remember the Road Runner cartoons – Wile E Coyote dashes off the edge of the cliff and keeps going, defying gravity. It's only when he looks down and realises there's no ground under his feet that he falls. The same is true in writing your initial draft. Don't stop, don't look down, keep pounding the keys and you'll get safely across.

"I was both a newspaper feature writer and sub-editor before branching into fiction and it taught me several useful lessons. The first is to write quickly, get your thoughts down while they're hot. Don't interrupt the flow or the chains of logic.

"Next, don't allow a blank screen to intimidate you. Slap some words down. You can always junk them later. Once you're off and writing you'll be surprised how quickly you're producing good stuff.

"Also, it's amazing how infrequently you need to rewrite. Even a piece that seems flawed can be easily improved – often by changing a few key words or switching the order in which sentences appear.

"Lastly, simplicity is always best. Simple words, simple stories, simply told have immense impact. Part of editing is removing overly elaborate expressions and unnecessarily baroque descriptions. Words are bricks – build stories with them, don't treat them like flowers to be arranged in a vase."

Iain's book *Cracking the Short Story Market* (ISBN: 978-1903119006) might help you get that first draft done without your inner editor sabotaging your efforts.

Lynne Hackles

For English writer and columnist Lynne Hackles, tuning out is second nature, something she had to learn as a child. "It's easy. I do exactly what I did with my mother when I was growing up," Lynne says. "I don't listen. Actually, the voice of the internal editor often sounded remarkably like my mother."

Sarah England

English short story writer and novelist Sarah England finds it hard to silence that internal editor. Easy to understand when you realise serials for magazines need to be submitted one installment at a time. In that sense there's no point finishing the entire project in one hit since basic building blocks can be rearranged by the magazine staff when you submit that first part of the story. Sarah says, "No, I cannot turn off the internal editor. What I do is write in bursts of energy while I am in the 'zone' or the head of a character. Then I'll edit it and move on. It is all instinctive. With a serial I usually have to get the first part absolutely right – and passed by the editor – then I'll do the rest. However, if I have to make changes to the first one I'll do so – and then send the whole thing to the editor. The magazine editor I work with tells me exactly what needs chopping and what had her confused."

Sarah mentions being "in the zone". If you're new to writing, you're probably wondering – perhaps with envy – how to actually get into that mind space. Try reading Natalie Goldberg's *Wild Mind* (ISBN: 978-0553347753) or *Writing Down the Bones* (ISBN: 978-1590302613), or Dorothea Brande's classic, *On Becoming a Writer* (ISBN: 978-0874771640). Another is *The Artist's Way* by Julia Cameron. Find a guide that speaks to you. Don't persevere with one you don't relate to.

John Floyd

US novelist and short story writer John Floyd reminds us that what works for you may not be the same as what works for others. "I try to get the whole first draft down on paper before thinking too much about any fine-tuning. I have writer friends who claim to edit 'as they go', so when they're finished they don't have to do any rewriting. That wouldn't work for me. During my editing/rewriting I often find myself going back and changing things that happened early in the story, which winds up changing things that happen later – so if I followed the edit-as-you-go process, I'd waste a lot of time and effort. I write it all down first, whatever the length and in all its ugliness – that's why they call them rough drafts, right? – and only then do I worry about the polishing and buffing."

Dani Collins

Time-poor writers like Canadian romance author Dani Collins see writing a shitty first draft as a luxury. "I turn off the internal editor to some extent. There are times where I know a scene is underwritten, but if things are flowing and only dialogue is landing on the page, I continue to write knowing I'll have to go back to flesh things out.

"At the same time, I'm on such tight deadlines I don't want to turn off the editor entirely. If I can save myself reworking something, I'd like to. My internal editor is like a base coach waving me along or telling me to hold up when necessary. As for techniques to shut off or control the inner editor, this takes practice. Write often enough and you'll develop confidence in the words you choose, but also in your process. You'll know when to trust something is good enough for now or when it's a pile of dreck you should untangle because you'll only have a bigger pile later if you don't.

"When I'm struggling to write a scene, it's often because I've taken a wrong turn and need to go back and fix something. There are times when I've soldiered through a scene that isn't working because I know what comes next, though. I think it comes down to whether you know how to fix the problem or if you need to think about it. I trust that if I go back in a day or two, revise from the beginning and hit that bumpy patch, I'll have a better idea how to resolve it. Learning to trust your own writing process is something that only comes with time."

Greg Barron

Australian novelist Greg Barron finds compromise works best for him. "I can turn off the internal editor by simply ignoring it. But I'm not totally sure I ever turn it off completely. You'll waste a lot of time if you write whatever comes into your head. I write as well as I can the first time, and if I know it's not working I'll back up and try again.

"Leigh Redhead said once that you have to trust the process, meaning you have to understand you can make your work better by redrafting. But crafting the novel as well as you can along the way will make the second draft easier, and the inevitable sense of despair will be easier to handle. The second draft is a terrible time for me. The fun's over, and as I read I realise just how much work there's still to be done. I start to enjoy things again a draft or two later."

Sue Moorcroft

A writer's personal and work backgrounds can also play a role in how they go about writing a first draft, as Sue Moorcroft explains. Sue is an English novelist and writer of short stories, serials, novella, columns, creative writing tutor and competition judge. "Using my layered writing technique, I can mentally postpone certain aspects because I know that they'll be dealt with later. Having been a secretary, a copytaker, a writer and a tutor, I'm constitutionally unable to leave spelling mistakes once I've noticed them, though. And, contrary to many writers, I do have both spellchecker and grammar checker switched on. It's not a perfect system but sometimes the technology highlights something I need to reconsider."

Christopher Currie

For writers like Australian Christopher Currie, technology plays an important role. Chris explains, "Turning off the internal editor is certainly something I've had to work on. It's a basic tenet you're taught in any writing course: *write first, ask questions later*. Which is not to say you should never reread what you've already written, just that you have to have confidence to keep going, and know you can always change it later. One the best things I've ever done is use a writing programme called Scrivener, which allows you to store all your drafts, scene breakdowns, research documents and, most importantly, your work in progress in a single document. This allows me to switch between them seamlessly, and means I can focus on one chapter or scene at a time, and reduces the temptation to *scroll back*, reread and re-edit."

Final thoughts

Feeling confused? Or liberated? The purpose of this chapter is simply to get you to write that first draft. Produce something that can be edited. As you can see, what works for one writer may not be what works for another. Your task is to discover what works FOR YOU – and DO IT.

First draft in hand, you're now ready to tackle that vital next stage – editing.

Why Edit?

Resist temptation

You've completed a first draft. Fuelled by a sense of achievement you want to immediately send your brilliant piece out into the world. Your finger hovers over the mouse, poised to email it to an editor.

But the other side of your brain, the bit that didn't write the story in the first place, steps in to ruin the party. And you may find yourself arguing with it.

Why edit? Why not just send this off and start something else?

The answer is *it's tough out there* in today's publishing world. An unpolished piece stands little chance. You have to make it as good as you possibly can. As US short story writer Kate Willoughby says, "You have to put your best foot forward because, if you don't, thousands of other writers are willing to go that extra mile."

Editing isn't optional

Editing isn't optional if you want to see your story in print. Learn how to do it and you'll save yourself a lot of heartache.

Does getting published matter to you?

If the answer is YES, you need to learn how to give your work that polish and sparkle that an editor will love.

Next time you're tempted to send out a first draft, thinking you don't have time to edit, STOP.

An editor doesn't have time to polish it for you.

Some will make an exception but this isn't the norm.

Jill Finlay, fiction editor of *The Weekly News* (UK) says, "I received a lot of stories from one woman. Her ideas were great, but her writing let her down. I took a couple and pointed out changes that had been made, but she didn't ever progress from there. I eventually had to say she needed to check her work, rewriting bits she felt could be improved, and I sent back a story to see what she came up with. I haven't heard from her since.

"It's hard telling people what you'd like them to do differently, as I realise how much time and effort goes into each story, but we have to select the best material for the paper.

"It'd be a shame to miss out on great stories, simply because one that maybe wasn't quite so unique was more polished, so I think the majority of writers are happy to embrace a few suggestions!"

Jill has accepted brilliant stories in the past, when they've contained basic mistakes. But those days are over. "I'd love to have time to correspond, tinker with stories and get well and truly stuck in, but it's simply not possible. I have less time to shape stories, and I have to choose the pick of the bunch from the off. So I'm less inclined to let something sloppy take the place of something tighter."

Motivated now? That brilliant first draft of yours needs to be worked on.

Leaving work to sit

The first step in editing is to put your work aside so you won't be blinded by its brilliance. In a week's time you'll see with painful clarity all the blemishes and sloppy writing. It can be discouraging. But it's something you need to do.

Ask any experienced writer.

How long do you need to wait before editing?

"The longer the better," according to English novelist and creative writing tutor Sarah Duncan. "But often there isn't as much time as I'd like. Sometimes I know what needs to be done and can get going straight away, but generally some distance helps. As I get more experienced, the distance gets shorter."

Finding time becomes tricky once you're working to tight deadlines.

Well-known Irish novelist Monica McInerney says, "In an

ideal world, I'd leave it to sit for a month or so. Longer, if I could. But I write a book every year or so, to tight deadlines, so there often isn't that luxury. But I find the editorial process – when I get feedback and notes from my different editors – is invaluable in helping me take a step back and see with fresh eyes what could be improved or tightened."

Australian novelist Greg Barron suggests switching to another writing project. "Before I was published I'd often have two books on the go, and work on one until I couldn't look at it anymore, then attack the other for a few months. Nowadays, I use publisher deadlines as natural breaks. This year, for example, my WIP needed to be sent to my publisher for a first look on June 1, then a completed draft on September 1. I then got it back again for a final edit until November 1. Each time I send it off I work on the next story until they email it back to me.

"You need time away. Fresh eyes are tremendously important and the only way to get fresh eyes – to stop thinking about it – is to work on something else, not just have a holiday."

Does the same advice apply to short story writers?

Teresa Ashby has had several thousand stories published. In her words, *"You must make time to edit.* If you've put all that work into writing something, then you owe it to yourself to make sure it's the best it can be."

Another much-published English writer, Della Galton agrees. *"If you don't have time to edit, you don't have time to write.* Editing is part of writing. Actually it can be a fun part – editing and polishing turn a rough draft into something glossy and beautiful. It's very satisfying."

John Floyd is an American writer with a thousand publishing credits to his name. Does he get it right first time? "I try to let a story sit and cool off after I've finished it. I don't have the patience to leave it alone for weeks, but I'll wait a day or two and then take what I hope is a fresh look at it. I always have several stories cooking at once, so I work on something else in the meantime. And yes, I have at times sent a story out before it was fully baked."

If you do send something out unedited, thinking you don't have time, and it's rejected, learn from the experience. Revise the story, polish it where you can, and try another market.

Or you could even resubmit to the original market, after a period of time. Editors love a writer who's prepared to learn from their mistakes.

Why can't the computer do it for me? Reasons not to use spellcheck

Computers come armed with all sorts of editing tools, high-lighting words and phrases to be changed.

Could a writer simply rely on this?

Writers aren't unanimous in their support of these tools. They can be a mixed blessing.

You could end up with more mistakes than you started with.

Take spellcheck, for example.

Teresa Ashby's advice is, "Never rely on spellcheck! And be careful if you decide to change a name or spelling by using find and replace. Although it's faster to do a blanket find and replace, you could end up with problems. For example, if you change Tom to Jack you could end up with words like jackatoes, accus-jacked and panjacktime."

Monica McInerney had a similar experience. "I don't use spellcheck, I do it manually. I was a proofreader in an earlier life, and pore over every word and line of my books before I send them back to my editors. Even so, an error always somehow manages to slip through. If I change a character's name midway through the writing process, I'll use the search and replace function to make the changes, but I do it one by one rather than a correct all. I learnt my lesson after changing a character's name from Max to Sam via auto-correct. I had to then go through line by line finding and fixing newly formed words like samimum and clisam!"

I've had this happen too. When I changed a character's name from Ian to something else, I quickly discovered how many words end in "ian".

Australian writer Greg Barron finds spellcheck useful. "I love the spellcheck-as-you-type and autocorrect functions, because they save time. Every time you mistype a simple word, it's fixed automatically. Misspelled words are underlined so you can either fix them as you go, or if things are flowing and you don't want to stop, you can come back later. I rarely use the formal spellcheckers these days. I also use find and replace functions all the time. I can't imagine how annoying it must have been to change a character's name in the bad old days of the typewriter. I have keywords that take me straight to the place I'm up to in the text, simply by searching for them, an invaluable tool when editing."

Different writers, different experiences.

As a first option, these editing tools can highlight problems. But nothing beats simply going through and considering each word or phrase separately. As John Floyd points out, some phrases a computer may object to are intentional on the author's part and add to the impact of the story. John says, "I like spellcheck, as long as I remember not to rely on it too heavily. I do NOT like grammar check programs, and I advise fiction writers to disable them. The problem with grammar check is that it flags things like sentence fragments, comma splices, split infinitives, run-on sentences, starting a sentence with a conjunction, ending a sentence with a preposition, and many other so-called errors that are sometimes a perfect fit for what I want to say. If Gene Roddenberry had relied on grammar-check, Captain Kirk would never have been able 'to boldly go where no man has gone before'."

Another issue is simply visibility of problems.

How many times have you read stories or chapters that you've written and not seen obvious spelling or grammar mistakes?

Things not picked up by the computer because they don't break any rules, but which are nonetheless glaring mistakes.

For example, I often type "fro" instead of "for", and am never contradicted by my laptop. John Floyd mentions an author who meant to write "does not" in her story, but put the space in the wrong place. Her spellcheck program happily okayed "doe snot".

How can you avoid these gaffes?

My answer is to print everything out and work through it manually. My eyes glaze over when I'm reading on-screen.

So I was pleased to learn from Sarah Duncan that there's scientific evidence to back this. "Editing is 75% more efficient when done on paper – you actually use a different part of your eyes and brain to edit using reflected light (paper) rather than emitted light from a screen. Print out your work and you'll spot far more errors. I always tell people that writing is cheap compared with, say, golf or skiing, so don't stint on paper and ink."

She also points out that the computer misses things like the overuse of certain phrases. "You have to be careful, especially with spellcheck – it misses some real clangers. I use the find and replace buttons a lot, it's useful if you know you repeat certain words or phrases, such as 'he sighed'. You can find every time you've used it, and give them something else to do apart from sighing!"

Where does this leave you?

Some writers are happy to use spellcheck and computer-generated grammar tools. Others avoid them completely.

Literary agent with Books & Such, Rachelle Gardner advises, "Everyone should use every tool at their disposal, always remembering your most reliable tool is your own eyes and brain. When you've spellchecked and edited to death, PRINT OUT your manuscript and go another round in hard copy. You'll be amazed what you find."

This view is shared by Jill Finlay. She sees mistakes in submissions that seem to result from a writer's reliance on spellcheck. "We don't use the 'z' version of spelling for 'realise' and spellcheckers tend to change automatically to that. I think they have their place, absolutely, as they can pick up mistakes that are hard to see on-screen.

I learned a sobering lesson at uni, though, as I submitted an essay that I'd spellchecked, but not actually read on paper after I'd printed it out. I was trying to start my sentence with: 'A linguistic commentary must....' And between autocorrect and spellcheck and my dodgy typing, the final version read: 'A linguistic nudist must...' My tutor wrote: 'Interesting image – but what's he/she doing here?!'

Take it from one who knows, spellcheck and autocorrect cannot and will not ever be able to read your mind. Be old-fashioned, print and read. Then have a cup of tea and read it all again!"

And if you still decide to use spellcheck, remember there are different versions. If you're writing for UK markets, you'll need to use English UK rather than English US.

Mistakes are inevitable

Let's say you do everything right, leaving your story to sit before editing, correcting the mistakes and polishing your work as best you can.

If you follow every piece of advice, does that mean there won't be any mistakes?

Sadly, no.

It seems inevitable that most published work will contain at least one mistake. Don't believe me? Read a magazine or newspaper. It won't be long before a mistake leaps out at you.

And if it's your work, don't be disheartened. You're in good company.

Della Galton says, "In one of the drafts of *How to Write and Sell Short Stories*, I mentioned a short tory instead of a short story. Not exactly the meaning I'd intended!"

Teresa Ashby admits, "I did a great deal of impulsive submitting at the start. I'd get something written and it'd be gone before the ink was dry. These days I hang on to things for too long before sending them off. It's possible to edit the life out of something and I don't think it matters how many times you read through your manuscript, you'll always find something to change. But a howler I found recently while editing was that I referred to a minor character having a family waiting for him at home then later talked about him living alone and having no close family. Although he was only a minor character that mistake really slapped me in the face!"

Jane Wenham-Jones says, "There's a howler in *Prime Time* despite it being checked by all sorts of people a zillion times. But as nobody but me seems to have noticed it yet (and I only did when I heard the audio version), I'll keep quiet!"

Sarah England says, "My funniest mistake was in a short story. I'd missed the 'w' key and slipped to the 's' key – so 'her face turned white with shock...' came out as 'her face turned shite with shock...' I had so nearly sent it to *My Weekly*..."

And Lynne Hackles confesses, "When I first began writing I sent out a children's story where the roof of the house was made of thatch yet, later, when the witch climbed up to it she slipped on the slates. That should've been tackled when editing but I didn't know about editing in those faraway days."

Mistakes are inevitable. Your job is to keep them to a minimum.

When Does Rewriting Stop and Editing Start?

When I put together this book proposal, I kept coming back to this basic question. *When does rewriting stop and editing start? And does it matter?* If we're going to work out a checklist for editing, then it does matter. What to include? What not to include? How much time do we need to set aside for the task?

Twelve writers have their say

Iain Pattison

"Rewriting is when I have to junk large sections of what I've written and start again. This happens when a scene doesn't work, perhaps because I'm telling it from the wrong character's viewpoint or I've misjudged the tone or pacing. It's when there's so much that jars or reads badly that it's easier to hit the delete button than waste time trying to rescue it.

"Editing is when I'm basically happy with what I've written but it needs tweaking and refining to make it shorter and slicker or give it more oomph or dramatic impact. That usually means removing lines of dialogue that don't earn their keep, ripping out unnecessary adjectives and adverbs, pouncing on repetition and slashing back descriptions that don't put over vital plot information but are there simply to look and sound pretty.

"I believe good writing has a natural flow – an almost musical rhythm – and it's amazing how one word too many or a phrase in the wrong place can spoil a story, like a bum note in a recital. To become a good writer you must develop an 'ear' for how words resonate. You must be able to hear the music.

"As easy way to think about the difference between rewriting and editing is to imagine you're cooking. Rewriting is required when what you take out of the oven is a smoking, blackened, carbonized mess that no one could possibly digest. Editing is the tasting and tweaking you do to make a good dish even more palatable – adding a pinch of salt, or thinning down an over-thick sauce, perhaps introducing a missing ingredient like a crucial spice or herb."

Sarah England

Novelist and short story writer Sarah England rewrites and edits at the same time, while her work is still in progress. "I write a few paragraphs usually before going over what I've written and altering it slightly. Then I continue until I have maybe written a chapter or most of a short story. Next day, with fresh eyes, I go over it all again and imagine I'm the reader. This time I may make significant alterations or add/subtract facts or information which came to me overnight. When the whole story/serial/chapter is written, I'll then go over it again. I consider this all as ongoing editing. I'll print it out and go over it in hard copy and then do a final edit. If it's a book, I find it easier to do it as I go along, so the task is never mountainous. That said, when *Expected* was put onto Kindle, I had to go through it all again looking for typos and along the way I made yet more changes.

"What do I think editing is? I think it's cutting out unnec-essary words, repetitions, superfluous information, excessive use of a name or repeated word, making the prose flow more smoothly, and correcting typos. That's what I try to do as I go along and then several times before checking the whole – in hard copy. Re-writing would be chopping out entire characters or sub-plots and putting in new ones. Also adding clues and moving the order of information around."

Simon Whaley

Simon Whaley writes both short stories and novels. He points out different editing is required when work is submitting to overseas editors. "For me, rewriting is what happens when my first draft fails to achieve what I wanted it to. That could be for many reasons: the resolution in a short story isn't right, or strong enough, or a novel's plot sags where it shouldn't. Once the text conveys what I want, editing begins. This is all about honing the text. It's where I consider total word length (more important for certain short story markets), point of view, style and vocabulary. If I have an idea that I feel might work for a different market, such as a short story that readers may enjoy in both a British and an Australian market, then I classify each piece as an edited version of the original draft because, essentially, the basic story is the same."

Sue Moorcroft

Writer and competition judge Sue Moorcroft doesn't differentiate between rewrites, revisions or tweaks. Sue says, "Once the first draft is down, to me anything after that is editing. I even edit as I write the first draft, typically by revising the work done in my previous writing session before moving forward. I like the editing/rewriting process more than the first draft process. It's like clay. Once I have it, I can mould it."

Jane Wenham-Jones

Jane Wenham-Jones writes pretty much everything. Novels, short stories, non-fiction, magazine columns, and even a pilot for a television show. She says, "I tend to rewrite as I go, in that I'm always rewording, cutting, pasting, fiddling with, as the piece or chapter unfolds. I see editing as the next stage – the getting-ready-for-publication. It's where you tighten, hone and polish and really think about the best possible choice of words and the cadence and rhythm of the language. It is, put quite simply, when you go back over what you have written in fine detail and make it the very best you possibly can."

Sheila O'Flanagan

Best-selling Irish novelist Sheila O'Flanagan differentiates between revising and editing, and raises the point that further editing is required once an independent copy editor has gone through her work. "I think you're rewriting when you're still making substantial changes to the plot, the characters and the action. Editing, however, leaves those basics unchanged but enhances them by providing additional context, cutting unnecessary elements and improving the general flow of the narrative. Finally, of course, there is copyediting which is when you get the manuscript back from an independent copy editor who looks for inconsistencies in the plot, action or descriptions as well as grammatical and punctuation errors."

Christopher Currie

Brisbane novelist and short story writer Christopher Currie explains how his view of editing changed once he'd worked with an editor. "Before the first time I worked with a professional editor on my first novel, the line was certainly blurred," Chris says. "I was a compulsive rewriter, and it certainly hindered the earliest drafts of my novel, in that I'd reread what I'd already written and rewrite it, thus stymieing any real sense of progress. Editing, as I understand it now, is something you do firstly yourself when you've finished a draft (i.e. reached a natural *endpoint* of your work), and then, more essentially, the act of someone else going through it and giving you initially structural, and then line by line feedback."

Greg Barron

Novelist Greg Barron offers the following analogy. "Rewriting is the process of getting the story right. It's like patting down a sandcastle to make it stronger so you can build it higher. It means deleting sections, writing new ones, changing names and situations so the story works.

"I often change locations, character genders, and even the point of the whole story before I'm satisfied. A lot of research usually goes in at this stage.

"Editing is more about fine tuning the text itself. Fixing up sentences, adding specific details, checking facts, expressing things more vividly, deleting adverbs and needless words. I tend to comb through the text on-screen first, then attack it in hard copy."

Peter Lovesey

Best-selling crime novelist Peter Lovesey effectively bypasses the rewriting stage by carefully planning the details of his novels before he begins writing. "A lot of the editing is done for me at the planning stage before I begin. I'm putting up ideas and testing them and usually rejecting them until I get a plot that pleases, with surprises and conflicts and characters the reader may identify with, as well as a satisfying mystery. After that the pleasure and the pain is all in the writing."

He sums up editing quite simply as "Getting it right". Adding, "My editor at the publisher's will point out any obvious gaffes, repetitions and discrepancies. I've usually been careful over research, but as an old hand in the writing game I'll sometimes use expressions that went out of fashion before I was born. So I'm glad that there's a process of reading and re-reading proofs to iron out all that stuff."

Monica McInerney

Well-known Irish novelist Monica McInerney says, "I think of rewriting as the process when I'm working on the first draft, when characters are still forming, the plot changing or heading in unexpected directions, which can mean going back to an earlier chapter to weave in the new threads. Editing is what happens after the first draft is done. Smoothing rough areas. Checking for consistency. Getting the rhythm right, the flow, the pace. You can't do that unless a complete first draft is finished."

Della Galton

Prolific English writer Della Galton points out another facet of editing. "If you're editing your own work these two things merge and are difficult to tell apart. However, if you're editing someone else's work there's a clearer distinction. I wouldn't actually add words to someone else's work, as I think it's easy to interfere with or change their voice. I'd cut words, sentences and possibly whole paragraphs, or I might change the order of sentences. But that'd be all. Rewriting would involve adding new material."

Lynne Hackles

Lynne Hackles has written short stories, several how-to books and an eBook for young cyclists. Lynne says, "I tend to do both rewriting and editing at the same time. I'll go through my first draft making changes to the plot, dialogue or character, changing words so that I am using the most suitable – all of which I consider rewriting – but, at the same time I am looking for missing or incorrect punctuation, spelling errors, incomplete sentences, factual mistakes – all of which I consider editing."

Final thought

As you can see, every writer has their own take on this. How you see editing depends on factors such as whether you're writing short stories or novels, whether your work is sent to an independent editor, and whether you're aiming your work at publishers in different countries. Dare I say it, it also reflects how far up the food chain you are, success-wise. There's a line between rewriting and editing but for each of us this line lies in a different place. It may also change throughout our writing career. What matters ultimately is that we engage in this process so that we send out our best work.

Part II

The Stages of Editing

The Stagesof Editing:
Substantive Editing

Editing is individual

Ask ten writers to describe their editing methods and you'll get ten different answers.

No one way is right. And no way is necessarily wrong.

Whatever your method, get the basics right and do things in the right order. There's no point polishing your language if the structure is falling down in places. Never polish a mess. Fix it first.

There are three stages or levels of editing.

1. **Substantive editing:** This covers every aspect of the overall structure – plot development, character portrayal, point of view, arrangement of scenes.
2. **Line editing:** This looks at style and continuity – consistency, choice of words, sentence construction.
3. **Copyediting:** This covers nuts and bolts details such as spelling and punctuation.

This chapter covers substantive editing.

Substantive editing: Fixing the overall structure

Substantive editing is where you get the building blocks of your story right. This is the first major edit where all the basics need to be examined. Major changes can be made. Nothing is out of bounds. Do whatever it takes to make your story compelling.

Examples of substantive edits:

a) You might decide to add an additional subplot.
b) A minor character may be given a stronger role – or dropped altogether.

c)   Scenes can be rearranged.

d)   You might leave out whole slabs of backstory, finding other ways to introduce the content. Award-winning author Hope Clark points out, "The biggest mistake made with backstory is telling it before the reader cares. Even in social settings, we're drawn to individuals way before we care where they're from, where they work, or where they went to school."

e)   New characters can be woven into the plot.

f)   You might decide to tell the story in the first person rather than third person.

g)   Viewpoint may need fine-tuning. The reader needs to know exactly who is speaking. Too much head hopping with different viewpoints can become confusing. Be careful to stay within the viewpoint character's head, only describing what could be experienced by that person. A character isn't able to know what someone else is thinking, for example. One way to test consistency is to rewrite the scene in the first person. Does it still make sense?

h)   Settings may need to be more clearly established.

How to go about substantive editing

One method is to print out the whole damn thing and arrange it on the floor in chapters or scenes. Some writers use highlighter pens or other colour coding so they can easily identify scenes written by different characters' point of view. It's a useful way of gauging if plot and character development proceed evenly and consistently. If the hero's main scenes in a romance are marked by blue cards, for example, it'll be evident if he's missing from five chapters in a row.

Similarly, scenes set in different locations or time frames can be colour coded. You'll be able to see at a glance how frequently you switch from one place or time to another.

Is your reader likely to be confused by the transitions? If they are, you're in danger of losing them.

Paying for a substantive edit
Sometimes it's worth paying an expert to undertake this stage of editing. Particularly with a first novel, it may be difficult for you to see what's lacking or where your plot could be strengthened. You can be too close and miss important problems.

If a literary agent has asked to read your completed manuscript and is impressed by your potential, you may receive what's known as an editorial letter, which essentially analyses the bones of your story, showing what changes are needed before it can be submitted to a publisher.

Plot holes are identified, problems in character development, pacing – anything that detracts from the page-turning quality of your work.

This includes advice on whether your story's structure is appropriate for the genre.

Examples:

Rachelle Gardner – Editorial letter
Literary agent Rachelle Gardner provides the following examples of advice she's given writers in an editorial letter:

"After reading 1/3 of the book, I'm still not quite engaged with the story. *I'm not sure what the major conflict is*; I don't know what's at stake for these characters; I'm not clear on who the antagonist is and what he wants. Consequently, I haven't begun to feel an excitement to see what happens."

"*Setting and story world*: This is a wonderful story that isn't grounded in any particular place or time. Most of the time I felt confused about the location as well as the time period. I can't tell if we're in the real world or a world of your making; are we in present day or the past or the future?"

"*Secondary characters*: I had a hard time differentiating between these two women. I found myself asking if one should be eliminated because they both serve the same purpose – simply being friends with your heroine."

"*What's at stake* for Lauren if she doesn't reach her goal? And along with that, what's at stake for others? For the world? If there's nothing to lose by not reaching her goal, there's no motivation for the reader to follow Lauren through this journey."

Hope Clark – Editing a novel

"Big picture changes have been huge as I wrote my novels. In *Lowcountry Bribe*, the first in my Carolina Slade Mystery series, four times I changed who killed who and how, and once the publisher received the manuscript, they asked me to change it again. I also wrote out a character and in the final edit with the publisher wrote another one in. And I added a pending hurricane to raise the tension since the story involved an outside search.

"In *Tidewater Murder*, my editor asked me to reverse two major action scenes, when I'd written one as a catalyst for the other. That alteration took me three straight days of rewrites.

"Reshaping doesn't just happen at the initial big picture level. It can change throughout. An author ought to be open to huge shifts and major rewrites at any stage. In my new pending series, I shifted from writing in first person to third, in order to get out of the head of Carolina Slade and better depict the voice of a different protagonist, Callie Jean Morgan. I also turned in the manuscript for the publisher to get concerned about using a real town as the setting, and was asked to consider making it a fictitious place instead - only three months before release!

"My final book is light years different from my first draft. Each edit, no matter how small, improves it, and often the smallest of ideas and concerns can cause monstrous shifts in the big picture. No matter how painful it feels, and yes I've cried over such changes, an author should remain open to whatever makes the book better . . . at any stage of the process."

Bruce Thomson – Editing a novel

"I finished the second draft of Across the Border some time last year. It needed another draft but I didn't feel like going through it again at that point. I thought I'd leave it for a year. In the meantime I've started a second novel.

"The first draft of *Across the Border* was 177,000 words. I wanted to get it down to 120,000 words at the most. I ended up at 107,000.

"It wasn't actually that hard and weirdly enjoyable. I knew at the outset that I'd overwritten so a lot of those dumped words were fluff. I'd often use 100 words to say something that could be said in 20. I also removed a character and a bunch of scenes with him. He was reasonably interesting but I was really using him as a prop. I removed three or four other chapters which didn't seem to contribute much to the overall story.

"I intend to play around with the structure in the third draft. It's set in two different timeframes. I've used a diary for some things that happened in the past but it feels clunky and contrived. I also might change it to first person because I feel more comfortable with that. I'm using it for the second novel and it feels right.

"The main thing I take out of this is that because it was my first attempt at a novel, I tried to throw too much into it."

Ginny Swart – Editing a magazine serial

"For my *People's Friend* serial, *Under the African Sun* I wrote a synopsis which I sent to the editors. I wanted to have the action divided between South Africa and the UK, and I had three age groups – teenagers, middle -aged and a wise grandmother, to take care of all the readership.

"They okayed it in principle and said each episode should be about 7000 words, be divided into three or four chapters and end with a cliffhanger. There was actually almost no interference from the editorial team once I got going.

"I spent some time sketching out each episode, going back and forth until I had a good idea of how it'd work out with the story being told over 11 episodes. They wanted 12 but I couldn't stretch it.

"I wrote a page of Chapter Outlines and stuck to these fairly well, although as ideas popped into my head I added a bit of action here and there.

"I made sure all the characters were mentioned or had some action in each episode. This was darned good training for a novel because, once I'd sent off the episode and they'd approved it, that was IT. No going back and adding stuff.

"I forced myself to keep writing without checking back every time I switched on my computer to re-read what I'd written the day before because it was tempting to fiddle and waste time. Before I submitted it, I'd go through the three chapters in the episode and check for things like the same adjective being used twice in the same chapter and that I hadn't changed names by mistake.

"I didn't print out as I went along mainly because my printer was slow so I just read onscreen. Once I'd sent them all off, I read the whole thing again (70,000 words) and found some errors which I listed, and they were able to change:

Mistakes: Episode 4 and episode 8 both begin with people swallowing hard! Please change
Episode 8 chapter 1: Dan says the boat is fitted with TWIN engines... make that fitted with a caterpillar diesel...

*Every ref to Heritage Society should be changed to Historical
Society*
*In Chapter 9 I renamed the boat Sea Freedom… please check this is
the same right through every episode.*

"I wrote each episode in about a week but often had to wait four
weeks for them to approve it. It was a good job I had those
chapter outlines to keep me on track or I would've forgotten
what I'd written!"

Tools

1. You need a second opinion – beta reader, literary agent,
   paid editor
2. Hone up on essentials. Useful how-to books include:
   Nancy Kress *Elements of Fiction Writing: Beginnings,
   Middles and Ends* (ISBN–13: 978-1599632193)
   Deborah Halverson *Writing Young Adult Fiction for
   Dummies* (ISBN-13: 978-0470945942)
   Debra Dixon *GMC: Goal, Motivation and Conflict: The
   Building Blocks of Good Fiction* (ISBN- 978-0965437103)

Tip: Last word

Always keep copies of your manuscript at each stage of editing.
You might need to re-introduce that deleted scene or character at
a later date.

Line Editing and Copyediting

Line editing: Fixing the general style

This stage irons out the inconsistencies in your story, in plot details, language and style. It examines sentence structure, choice of word, and continuity in detail.

If your heroine has blue eyes in chapter one, they shouldn't be green by chapter eight. Don't laugh. These mistakes can and do happen. Ask any editor.

When a writer changes a character's name, there are often a few remaining instances where their original name is used.

Details can become confused. If you add a subplot where there's a car crash, the hero can't drive that same car that same day.

You'd be surprised how many inconsistencies appear in stories. And the longer the story or novel, the greater their likelihood.

They need to be fixed. You don't want your reader scratching their head over a silly mistake when they're meant to be swooning over the hero or sitting on the edge of their seat. "But isn't that the car that just got written off?" isn't what you want them saying. You've lost them if this happens.

You don't want to put your reader to sleep either. That means varying the way your sentences are constructed. A paragraph where every sentence begins with "She..." will make your reader yawn.

Varying pace is important. Generally speaking, short sentences create dramatic tension. Henning Mankell's *Wallander* novels exemplify this. Save your flowery prose for descriptive scenes.

Read your dialogue out loud. Is it believable?

Are transitions from one point of view to another clear or is your reader going to wonder who on earth is speaking?

Essential skill: Reducing word count

Literary agent Rachelle Gardner advises, "Most writers can significantly shorten their manuscript by eliminating extraneous adverbs, adjectives, gerunds, and passive verbs. If you cut 10 words per page in a 350-page manuscript, you've shortened it by 3,500 unnecessary words.

"Here's a checklist of things to consider cutting:

- Adverbs, especially those with "ly" endings. Ask yourself if they're necessary.
- Adjectives. Often people use two or three when one or none is better.
- Gerunds. Words that end in "ing."
- Passive voice: Over-use of words like "was," "were" and "that" indicate your writing may be too passive. Reconstruct in active voice.
- Passages that are overly descriptive.
- Passages that describe characters' thoughts and feelings in too much detail, such as long sections of narrative or interior monologue.
- Passages that tell the reader what they already know.
- Unnecessary backstory.

"Here's a list of words to watch for: *about, actually, almost, almost, like, appears, approximately, basically, close to, even, eventually, exactly, finally, just, just then, kind of, nearly, practically, really, seems, simply, somehow, somewhat, sort of, suddenly, truly, utterly, were.*

"Make use of the search and replace function in Word if there are specific words you tend to overuse.

"Once you go through this exercise, you'll find your manuscript remarkably cleaner. Remember, no matter how many words you cut, your editor will always find more."

Just be sure not to make any fresh mistakes in the process.

Examples:

Ginny Swart – Losing or adding words

Ginny says, "I do a lot of chopping! I have loads of stories that started life at 2000 words and went down to 1500 to suit the word count.

Down by the Riverside started out as 3000 words for UK *Woman's Weekly*. Here's an excerpt, which is 295 words:

Then this term I meet Dominic Hunt at Jodie's party. He is hanging around the doorway, checking out the dancing, not talking to anyone. He is very tall and sort of intense, with thick dark eyebrows that almost meet in the middle and he doesn't smile much. He doesn't move at all in fact, and it's his stillness that makes him kind of magnetic.

I can't help it, I walk up to him and say, "Hi, my name's Alison."

And he looks down at me and says, "Okay."

I should just walk away but I say, "So what's yours?"

"Dominic."

I stand next to him, feeling a bit silly but unable to move off. Then he says, "Boring party, want to split?"

His dark brown eyes look right into mine and all I can say is, "Yes. Fine."

And I get the feeling that this is not a very smart thing to do. Dominic is exactly the kind of guy my mother would disapprove of, which is probably why I agree to go with him.

He has a nice big car, better than most boys' old jalopies, and we go to a coffee shop in town and sit at a table in the corner. I think he must be at least twenty-five, and he's completely different from any guy I've dated before. He has a ponytail and wears a long old-fashioned black coat, which adds to his unusual appearance.

We sit in silence for a bit. He just looks at me from under his black eyebrows and I start to feel uncomfortable so I say, "What do you do, Dominic? Are you studying?"

"I study life. In all its crazy, hopeless permutations." He looks at me as if challenging me to argue.

When I needed to shrink this story to 2000 words, I edited this part down to 161 words:

Then this term I meet Dominic at Jodie's party. He's hanging around the doorway, not speaking. He is tall and sort of intense and his stillness is almost magnetic.

I say, "Hi, my name's Alison."

And he looks at me and says, "Okay."

I should just walk away but I say, "So what's yours?"

"Dominic."

I stand next to him, unable to move off. Then he says, "Boring party, want to split?"

His dark brown eyes look right into mine and all I can say is, "Sure. Fine."

We go to a coffee shop and sit at a table in the corner. He's at least twenty-five, dead romantic- looking. He has a ponytail and wears a long old- fashioned black coat which adds to the effect.

He just looks at me from under his black eyebrows and I feel uncomfortable so I say, "What do you do, Dominic? Are you studying?"

"I study life. In all its crazy permutations."

Iain Pattison – Line editing a short story

"I don't consciously have an editing checklist. I simply read through a story time and again, nibbling away at what I can remove and reading it out loud to identify what sounds clumsy. Before I send out a piece I may have made a dozen or more editing runs through it. Each time I spot something new to cut or amend.

"My aim is always to achieve maximum impact with minimum words. By the time I send out a story it may have lost a third of its length. Something that amuses me is when people say: 'The story slot in the magazine is 1,000 words but I can't get my yarn down beyond 1300 words.' I know if I got my hands on their piece it'd end up at 850 words! Editing is about knowing what's vital and what isn't; being ruthless. It's a terrible cliché, but you DO have to kill your darlings.

"I'm never content with what I write and if a story hasn't done as well as I'd hoped in a competition, I'll re-edit it before resubmitting elsewhere. When I read any of my work that's published in anthologies or magazines, I still yearn to re-edit it. It may only be changing one word – but to me that dud word leaps off the page screaming for attention.

"One thing I do fixate on is repetition. We all have favourite words and phrases and it's easy to overuse them. For me it's the word *but*.

"Repeating words makes writing flat, dull and predictable. An important tool in combatting this is the thesaurus. After I've done a first draft, I use this to find as many alternative expressions as possible to the stale ones I've allowed to creep in. Another must-have book for me is a dictionary."

Hope Clark – Avoid repetition

"Don't assume you repeat the same words in each of the works because I've found that no two stories are the same in the words I like to overuse. In my most recent manuscript it's *hand, look, rose, understand, thought* and *stood*."

Tools for line editing

"Create a style sheet," advises literary agent Rachelle Gardner. Editors create one when they line-edit or copyedit your book. Rachelle says, "It's their responsibility to ensure everything is as correct and consistent as possible so, as they're editing, they write down details; names of people, places, businesses and all proper nouns; unusual spellings; and style rules that will apply to your manuscript.

"Your style sheet doesn't need to be formal or detailed. A simple one that you create as you write or revise could help you define and keep track of elements that are important to you.

"When editors create style sheets, they include:

a) *A list of important style rules* that will be followed throughout the manuscript. Note which dictionary and style guide you're using. The important thing is consistency and a pleasant reading experience. This section addresses things like whether or not the serial comma is used; under what circumstances kinship or pet names ("mama" or "sweetheart") are capitalised or lowercased; whether inner thoughts are set in italics or roman type; whether to spell out numbers or use numerals; and countless other issues that come up in editing.

b) *The book's setting* – time frame and location on the map.

c) *A list of all the places and street names,* to ensure consistency in spelling and capitalisation. For instance, is it Babies 'R' Us… or Babies R Us? Is it Wal-Mart? WalMart? Walmart?

d) *A list of all the people in the book* with the correct spellings of their names. You'd be amazed how often a writer spells the same name three different ways throughout a book. If personal details about the person are included, you may want to note those also, such as age, relationship to another person, hair colour, eye colour, height and any other information.

e) *A long list of words* whose spellings could be easily mistaken or challenged. For example, "blonde" and "blond" are typically confused. A nicely edited manuscript requires a rule so the word is spelled consistently, such as blonde for female and blond for male; or blonde for noun and blond for adjective. Sometimes a word is only used once, but is included in the style sheet to show an intentional decision has been made to go with a certain spelling; or to show the spelling has been verified through an external source. For example, "Walmart" is verified by the company's website.

"If you're self-publishing, it's important to keep a style sheet, so you can communicate your choices to the editor you hire. In traditional publishing, it's a good idea because it helps you stay consistent, and will also help your publisher see that you've made intentional style decisions that they shouldn't change."

Copyediting: Fixing the nuts and bolts

By this stage, all the structural changes have been made, details of character, time and setting are consistent and your story is well paced. Now is the time to weed out spelling mistakes, misuse of punctuation, and correct any grammatical errors. The chapter "Common Editing Mistakes to Avoid" covers this in detail. Sometimes facts will need to be checked at this stage. Any overly long sentences or paragraphs need to be made more reader friendly. Remove any words that can be cut.

Tools for copyediting

1. Style manual: For example, *The Chicago Manual of Style* (ISBN-13: 978-0226104201)
2. Style guide: For example, BBC Style Guide, available online at http://www.bbc.co.uk/academy/journalism/news-style-guide.
3. Grammar book: For example, *The Cambridge Grammar of the English Language* (ISBN – 9780521431460)
4. Punctuation book: For example, *Penguin Guide to Punctuation* (ISBN: 9780140513660)
5. Dictionary

Checklist

Doing things in the right order

The three-tiered approach to editing works. Begin by fixing the overall structure of your story or novel. Scenes, characters, pacing, viewpoint and setting all need to be as strong and well crafted as possible. Once the bones are right, and only then, work through the layers of details and language. There's no point doing it the other way around. You'll only double your workload.

When you make basic changes it affects the whole work. For example, you may be putting the finishing touches by checking commas and notice a disproportionate amount of dialogue in some scenes. Once you've made this kind of change you're back to square one.

Substantive editing – Fixing the overall structure

Characters

Is it clear who the main character is (particularly if you use multiple viewpoints)? What their purpose or goal is? Do they face enough challenges?

Do you know your characters well enough?

Are there any clichéd characters? Can original touches be added to round out any of the characters?

How are characters introduced? Try to show them in action rather than tell us who they are.

Do you describe the characters – or let their actions speak for themselves? Do you say someone is angry or show them throwing a plate?

Do you introduce too many characters at once?

Are characters' names well chosen?

Do several characters have names beginning with the same initial?

Too many hyphenated names can become confusing. Names that are universally plain can be a problem too.

Names that weren't used in that particular era can be confusing.

There's no need to name every single character. Omit names for ones who aren't important to the plot.

Does every character earn their place in the story?

Is there a character who could be omitted without detracting from the story?

Could two characters be amalgamated into one without losing anything?

Does any character demand a stronger role?

Would adding a new character strengthen the novel/story? Perhaps a confidante for your hero or heroine?

What's at stake for your characters? Are they in danger of losing something that matters to them?

Does every character want something?

Do the needs/wants of the main characters shape the plot?

Is there enough conflict?

Does your main character change by the end of the story? Have they evolved as a person?

Do we care enough about the characters? Are they interesting enough?

Scenes

Does your story have a definite beginning, middle and end?

Is there a subplot?

Does the story open with a strong hook? Does each chapter end with a hook?

Would the story be stronger if the first scene were omitted?

Are scenes presented in the right order? Could more conflict/ tension be created by rearranging them?

Can any scenes be omitted?

Is groundwork laid for later plot developments?

Is back-story woven in seamlessly? Are there info dumps? Could these details vital be conveyed in other ways such as dialogue or interior monologue?

Do characters disappear from too many consecutive scenes? If you're writing a romance, the hero and heroine need to stay on stage most of the time.

Point of View

Is it always clear who is speaking?

Is there too much head hopping? How often do you alter point of view?

Do you alter viewpoint character at a natural break such as the end of a chapter, rather than midway through which can confuse a reader?

Would your story be stronger if you changed the viewpoint character?

Would the story be more compelling if written in the first person instead of third?

Does your viewpoint character know things they couldn't know? See things they couldn't see?

Setting

Is your story set in a recognisable well-described place/s? Time period?

Is it clear exactly when each scene occurs? This is particularly relevant if your story is set in different time frames.

Are transitions from one setting to a different one seamless so readers know exactly where they are and when?

Do you use different senses to describe locations?

What's the role of your setting? Does it affect your characters?

Pacing

Are short sentences used to build tension? Are longer descriptive ones used to slow the pace? Too much of either can bore your reader.

Does the story sag in places?

Does too much happen in too short a time frame?

Plot holes

Are there any gaps in the plot? Is it clear how A leads to B? You may need to add a scene so one action logically follows another.

Line editing – Fixing the general style

Sentence structure

Is sentence structure varied? Watch for several consecutive sentences beginning with 'he' or 'she' or 'I'.

Are there too many consecutive short sentences? Are there too many consecutive long sentences?

Are there too many consecutive sentences which begin with a long phrase?

If it's hard to read out loud, it needs to be changed.

Details of character and plot

Check plot details for continuity if you've changed scenes.

Are your character descriptions consistent?

Where a character's name has changed, does the original name still appear anywhere?

Is a character referred to by different names? Perhaps a first name to begin with, then later by surname, or both? This can be confusing.

Dialogue

Check your dialogue is natural and believable. Read it aloud.

Simplify tags if necessary. 'Said' is fine. Are there places where they can be left out? Are there places where they're needed? Is there ambiguity? If there are several men speaking, it's not enough to use 'he said'.

Do you have characters doing something impossible? For example, "How are you?" he smiled.

Avoid heavy use of dialect. It can make a story hard to read.

Is there a balance between dialogue and narrative?

Do characters mention something they both know simply because you need to convey this information?

Do characters use each other's names too often in dialogue?

Adjectives and adverbs

Make sure your manuscript isn't top heavy with your favourite adverbs and adjectives. Question the inclusion of any word ending in –ly. Try to replace them with a stronger verb. 'She spoke loudly' can become 'She shouted'.

If you have two adjectives before a noun, choose the stronger one and delete the other.

Note that stories in women's magazines often use adverbs so check your target publication.

Clichés

Clichés are best avoided. Find your own metaphors and similes.

Passive voice

Try to avoid using passive voice. Watch for overuse of "was", "were" and "that".

Show don't tell

Readers like to work things out for themselves. Don't spell it all out. Leave something to the imagination.

Physical senses – sight, touch, smell, taste, sound

Include several senses when you describe a character or scene.

Readability

How does your story/chapter look on the page? Is there white space to break it up? Solid print consisting of long paragraphs can look unwelcoming to a reader.

Copyediting – Fixing the nuts and bolts

Check for spelling mistakes. Be careful of words that look similar but have different meanings – for example *affect, effect*

Punctuation – for example *its, it's*

Grammatical errors – for example, misusing *their, they're, there*

Are there any misplaced modifiers? Make sure each phrase is as close as possible to the noun or pronoun it describes.

Is it clear which noun a pronoun refers to?

Are there any commas that aren't necessary? These can slow a sentence down.

Check facts.

Tip

When you've worked through this checklist, put your manuscript away.

Come back to it later with fresh eyes and do it all again.

Common Editing Mistakes: Punctuation

Put your work in the top 10%

I asked magazine editors, competition judges and a literary agent to list the common editing mistakes they regularly see. Iain Pattison sums up the view from the other side of the desk. "At least 90 percent of all competition entries I judge cry out to be edited. There are obvious spelling mistakes, missing or incorrect punctuation, terrible sentence construction, grammatical errors and shoddy layout."

In other words, avoiding these mistakes would put your work in the top 10 percent.

The most common mistake is using incorrect punctuation.

Incorrect punctuation:

Apostrophe

Error: Leaving out an apostrophe that's needed
Competition judge Sue Moorcroft says, "People say they can't be bothered with apostrophes and omit them. But *Hell be with you soon* has quite a different tone and meaning to *He'll be with you soon.*"

Explanation:

1. An apostrophe shows ownership. For example: *The man's car.*

2. An apostrophe is used when two words are joined together to form one word. It takes the place of the letter/s left out.

Error: Using an apostrophe to indicate plural
Jill Finlay, fiction editor of *The Weekly News* (UK) gives an example.

"Someone wrote a great Christmas story but was convinced the plural of *tree* was *tree's*. It just about made me weep."

As competition judge Jane Wenham-Jones says in her entertaining guide *Wannabe a writer?* "Nobody's going to take you seriously if you think potatoes has an apostrophe."

Comma

We've all seen articles like "Is the comma dead?" It isn't and writers need to know where to put a comma and where not to put one.

Below are some of the worst offences. When in doubt, use a style guide. Most publishers have a manual they use as a reference.

And while you're reading it, check their use of inverted commas. Some use single, others like double. Editors prefer writers who notice these things.

Dialogue

There are different norms for setting out dialogue, depending on whether you're writing for a British or an American audience. The biggest complaint is that writers are inconsistent. Better to choose one form and stick with it.

Error: Leaving out a comma before a form of address

English writer Della Galton gives an example: "Would you like to eat, Grandma?" has a very different meaning to, "Would you like to eat Grandma?"

Error: Not knowing whether to put punctuation inside or outside closing inverted commas

Competition judge Lynne Hackles says, "The most common problem is punctuation when using dialogue. Many would-be competition winners aren't sure if punctuation should go inside or outside the closing inverted commas. In many entries, to be on the safe side, the writer has used both ways, punctuation inside and outside. Some have even carefully alternated it."

Example:

Here's an example of correct setting out of dialogue, taken from my story *Tess is Leaving* (*Woman's Weekly Fiction Special*, Issue 6, 2012):

> *"Mum, I've decided to spend the next six months backpacking around Europe."*
>
> *My mind immediately filled with practicalities. "What about your job? What about your dancing classes?" And finally, "What about Sam? Is he going too?"*

Error: Incorrectly punctuating dialogue

There are several instances where a comma is needed in dialogue.

Example: He asked "Where is the nearest supermarket?"

Correction: He asked, "Where is the nearest supermarket?"

Explanation: A comma is needed to separate dialogue from the rest of the sentence.

Error: Not using a comma correctly in a list

Example: She packed her sunscreen, beach towel, sandals, and sunglasses.

Explanation: In a list, a comma is used to replace the word "and". Where "and" is used, a comma is not needed.

Error: Placing a comma between a subject and its verb

Example: The problem, is that I am too tall.

Explanation: A verb is not normally separated from its subject.

Final Tips:

Remember that when using commas to surround phrases, those phrases can be removed and the sentence still makes sense.

Some say commas should go anywhere you need to take a breath. Ignore this. That'd mean asthmatics would use far more commas than those who can breathe easily.

Exclamation mark

Error: Overusing

Example: Teresa Ashby says, "Recently I was editing an old manuscript and I was appalled by the amount of exclamation marks I'd used. I replaced them all with full stops then, when I read through the whole thing, I only put back two."

Question mark

Error: Misplacing a question mark, or leaving it out when it's needed

It's easy enough to put question marks at the end of a sentence in prose. But what about in dialogue? Where does it belong? And what happens if it's not dialogue but a question in someone's thoughts?

Example:

1. She asked whether the croissants were baked yet.
2. "Are the croissants baked yet?" she asked.
3. Were the croissants baked yet, she wondered?

Incorrect use of common pronouns:

Its, it's

Error: Using the incorrect form

Explanation: *Its* is a possessive pronoun. Only. It can't be used as a subject.

It's = it is. The apostrophe is used because the letter "i" is left out.

It's can also be used as an abbreviation for "It has".

Example: *It's* clear that the lorikeet is upset. Look how it's plucking out its chest feathers.

Your, you're

Error: Using the incorrect form

Explanation: *You're* = you are. The apostrophe is used because the letter "a" is left out.

Your is a possessive pronoun. Only. It can't be used as a subject.

Example: *You're* going to love the piano lessons *your* uncle has arranged for you.

They're, their, there

Error: Using the incorrect form

Explanation: *They're* = they are. The apostrophe is used because the letter "a" is left out.

There = place

Their = a plural possessive pronoun

Example:

1. *There* is going to be a party at *their* house tonight.
2. *There* are thousands of stars visible in the sky tonight. *They're* gleaming brightly.

Note: Don't assume autocorrect will get this right. Twice in a story I'm writing my laptop has made ungrammatical suggestions. It wanted me to change *there* to *they're* in the following: "This was hardly the time or place to talk things through. Especially with the doctor there." And in "It was Friday evening, their busiest", autocorrect suggested *they're busiest*.

Never be afraid to ignore your computer's suggestions. Chances are you're the one who's right.

That, who

Error: Using "that" when it should be "who"

Explanation: "Who" refers to a person, "that" refers to a non-person.

Example: Wrong – He is the man that burgled my uncle's house.

Correct – He is the man who burgled my uncle's house.

Who's, whose

Error: Using the incorrect form

Explanation: "Who's" is used when the meaning is "who is" or "who has".

Example: *Who's interested in playing tennis?*

Who's stolen my jam tart?

The apostrophe is used to represent the missing letter/s.

whose = possessive pronoun

Example: *Whose* hat is this?

Common Editing Mistakes:
Structure and Style

The following errors in structure and style are commonly found in work submitted to magazine editors. Improve your chances of success by eliminating them from your work.

Repetitive sentence structure

Error: Every sentence is simply structured without variation

Example: Samantha Hazell, lead editor of the Trues magazines in the US says, "Some writers submit stories that are plagued by simple sentence structure. The repetition of subject + verb, subject + verb, makes the story read amateurish and slow. We encourage writers to vary their sentence structure when we issue rewrites."

Story structure

Error: Info dump on page one

Example: Competition judge Iain Pattison says, "Structural problems are common. Some writers waste the first page setting the scene, giving lengthy and unnecessary description of the main character or the setting. They don't actually start their narrative until page two."

Error: Uneven pace

Example: Iain Pattison says, "Some writers leave things to the last minute and knock out a story just hours before the competition closes. It's only when they've eaten up three quarters of the allowed word count that it dawns on them they're only half way through their plot. There isn't time to do anything about it so they squeeze the remaining storyline into a few sentences, making the ending seem staccato, disjointed and thrown together.

"These entries are easy to spot – always uneven in tone and pace, with a rushed and unsatisfactory ending that grates with the smooth and enchanting opening. Of course, they never win.

"I've even seen one entry where the writer stopped when she reached the word limit and sent notes explaining how her story WOULD have concluded!"

Lack of continuity

Error: Essential details changing during the course of a story

Example: Editor Samantha Hazell says, "Oftentimes, I see plot-driven mistakes. The colour of a dress might change or the name of a restaurant. The female lead's name might be Anna for the first half of the story and then change to Annie. Timelines are the worst to keep track of. It'll be Wednesday in the story and a character will reference an appointment they have for Saturday. But the next day the character will attend that appointment. It's hard to keep track of so many details, but any good editor can help you identify these common mistakes."

Example: Iain Pattison finds "people arriving back from journeys before they've set off or knowing vital pieces of information about events they didn't witness and no one else told them about."

Confusing dialogue

Error: Failing to differentiate between speakers so reader is left uncertain who is actually talking

Liz Smith, fiction editor at *My Weekly* speaks of "confusing dialogue with no stage directions to give the reader a clue to who is speaking". This mistake often arises when writers trim their stories to a specified word count by losing speech tags.

Use of weasel words

Error: Using words that don't add anything

Explanation: You know it's a weasel word if it can be left out without changing the meaning. Using too many adverbs and adjectives fits this category.

Examples: Literary agent Rachelle Gardner provides the following list: *about, actually, almost, like, appears, approximately, basically, close to, even, eventually, exactly, finally, just, just then, kind of, nearly, practically, really, seems, simply, somewhat, sort of, suddenly, truly, utterly, were.*

American writer John Floyd adds another. "An error I see often in students' manuscripts is the needless use of *that*. Example: I heard that she likes you."

And in *Wild Mind*, Natalie Goldberg urges us to leave out the words *because, very* and *really*.

Overwriting

Error: Needless repetition

Example: John Floyd notes, "Beginning writers tend to repeat everything, not only by accident but also because they're trying to make everything absolutely clear. This kind of overwriting is distracting, and pulls the reader out of the story. And repetition doesn't necessarily mean typing the same word twice. A sentence like *"Come here," he demanded* is repetition, because the word 'demanded' is redundant."

Passive voice

Error: Using passive voice when active is better

What is passive voice? Why is it considered a mistake?

Passive voice means writing as something is happening, in a descriptive way rather than an immediate one.

Here's an example:

The Belgian chocolates were being given to the injured girl by her boyfriend, Peter.

Note the words 'were' and 'being'. Parts of the verb "to be" often indicate passive tense.

Here's the same sentence written in active voice:

Peter gave Belgian chocolates to his injured girlfriend.

Remember, magazine editors prefer a greater sense of

immediacy. Check your stories for the verb 'to be' + a past participle. Substitute action verbs.

Wrong use of tenses

Error: Changing verb tense in mid-sentence
Verbs establish when action takes place, whether past, present or future. The tense needs to be consistent or readers become confused.

Liz Smith commonly sees this in *My Weekly* submissions.

Unnecessary changes of viewpoint

This is another common problem in submissions to *My Weekly*.

Changing viewpoint within a short story can be confusing. A reader must feel oriented. If they're experiencing events through the viewpoint of a particular character, this must remain consistent.

Again, a viewpoint character is essential within a novel. While some successful novelists change viewpoint character within scenes – and do it convincingly – it's generally better to stick with one viewpoint character per scene.

Word length

Error: Not abiding by guidelines regarding length
Example: Liz Smith says, "I'm restricted by the length of stories I can use so it's pointless sending a story more than 100 words over the guideline length."

Similarly, novelists need to consider what word length is preferred for their genre.

Setting out

Error: Not adhering to publication's guidelines
Example: Fiction editor Jill Finlay has limited time for choosing and editing a story. She must choose ones that adhere to specifications. That is, whether to have indented paragraphs, single or double spacing, the size of margins, preferred font and so on.

Where formatting isn't specified, stick with the tried and true. For submissions to US publications, for example, use William Shunn's *Guide to Proper Manuscript Format*, available online.

A boring title

Readers have short attention spans. Your story or novel needs a pick-me-up-and-read-me title.

My Uncle Kevin told me about a businessman who believed he sold the best jeans at competitive prices. But nobody bought them. The shop was called *Jeans*. In a moment of inspiration he changed the name to *Below the Belt*.

You guessed it. Business immediately picked up.

Learn from this. Make yours the title that catches an editor's eye.

Note changes made by editors. They reflect the tastes and expectations of their readers. For example, my title *Did you forget to tell me?* was changed to *A Question of Attitude* for *My Weekly*, but a South African editor retained my title. *Pumpkin Scones and Petits Fours* was renamed *Home from Home* by *People's Friend*.

Dangling modifier

Rule: Place an adverbial phrase or clause as close as possible to the verb it modifies.

Otherwise the meaning can be confused.

For example, whose innocence is in question in the following?

If found innocent, the barrister could recommend the accused sue for defamation.

The correct version is:

If the accused is found innocent, the barrister could recommend he sue for defamation.

Conclusion

Will your work be taken seriously if it contains any of these common mistakes?

Competition judge Sue Moorcroft sums up the general consensus. "I see a lot of stories that are inadequately or wrongly punctuated, or there are spelling or grammar mistakes. It's often obvious where the writer has relied upon spellchecker, because homophones are confused: *down at heal* instead of *down at heel*, for example. These errors can stem from dyslexia or from interrupted education, so I don't disqualify on that basis.

"That said, I'm a passionate believer in good spelling, grammar and punctuation and misuse of any of these things can lead to confusion or to jerking the reader out of the story. Therefore, a badly edited story will appear to be poorly written, and won't impress me. The easier a story is to read and appreciate, the more likely it is to score well."

Will these mistakes cost you a contract or an acceptance?
Not necessarily. But editors and judges agree that if two pieces are of equal merit, it is always the one with accurate grammar and punctuation that's chosen.

Iain Pattison says, "If I read two rival entries where the storytelling is of equal skill and charm, I'll pick the well-edited and well-presented narrative over the one that's ragged around the edges."

It's a question of being professional, as Jill Finlay points out. "If you're submitting work in the hope of securing payment, I see that as a professional agreement and therefore you need to present yourself and your writing as well as you can. Grammar, punctuation and spelling – where do I begin? You're using language to tell a story, so you must use that language correctly. Mug up on apostrophes – its/it's and no apostrophes for plurals. It's amazing how many people seem in the dark about it – or think it's irrelevant – but language is your tool. Use it wisely! It really does make a difference in meaning and how you appear to an editor."

How do you wish to appear?

Ragged around the edges or polished and easy to read?

Work your way through these common bugbears and you'll find yourself in the top 10%.

Part III

Editing in Practice

Novelists Explain
Their Editing Techniques

We've looked at the three main stages of editing. Common editing mistakes are identified. And a checklist has been created that covers the entire editing process. Now let's see how this works in practice. Real writers, real editors, real pieces of fiction.

Part III contains examples of how writers edit, how editors edit, and how one book was edited from first draft to final submission.

This chapter deals with novelists.

The unpolished first draft

Your first draft is finished. Step One in the path to being published. Now for Step Two. Editing.

How do you go about editing something as large and unwieldy as a novel? It could be 500 pages or it could be 200.

I asked eight novelists what they do. Each has a different approach. Read them and think what you can take away from their methods.

Let's begin with UK writer, Simon Whaley as his methods involve time management skills and are user-friendly.

Simon Whaley – Editing scene by scene

"The first thing I do is to print out the whole text – not with a view of editing it on paper but just to read it. If I were to do this on screen I'd be tempted to tinker and edit as I saw things. For me, this stage is all about getting to know my text again. I simply read through, jotting down any thoughts or comments. I record which scenes have plot holes or where character descriptions don't tally. I may decide new scenes are needed or entire scenes can be deleted. Essentially I create a checklist of things that need doing. During this process I often surprise myself with what I read. By the time you get to the end of the first draft you're elated with the achievement but then doubts creep in. Is it any good? It's only by sitting down and reading the whole text that I get that complete overview. Don't get me wrong – I often find bits that are truly awful, but things are never as bad as I sometimes imagine them to be. We can be our worst critics.

"Once I've done that, I go through my checklist making the necessary structural changes. Then I begin my in-depth editing process. This is where I check spelling, punctuation, grammar, style and the choice of words. I do this on screen. My novels are written in clear, distinct scenes, so that's how I edit: one scene at a time. This helps turn the process into a manageable exercise. Whilst each scene varies in length, I set myself a target of editing so many scenes at a time. Sometimes I set a daily target whilst on other occasions I set a weekly target. It depends what else I'm doing that week. Even if I think I'll only be able to edit one scene a day, that's the target I set. By editing on a scene-by-scene basis I make the editing process more manageable, and psychologically that makes it easier to cope with!"

(For more advice and insights on time management, see Simon's *Positively Productive Writer*, ISBN 978-1-84694-851-0)

Peter Lovesey – Editing sentence by sentence

Best-selling crime writer Peter Lovesey has had over 40 novels published. His success shows his methods suit his writing. That doesn't mean they'll work for you, as he'll be the first to tell you. "Let me say at the start that I don't recommend my way of working. I'm a Virgo. Can't leave a sentence until I'm happy with it. It's slow, slow, slow."

Peter doesn't work in drafts. He aims to get it right first time around. Each morning when he sits down to write, he looks at yesterday's efforts to get back in the mood he had when he wrote it. Is much editing needed at this stage? "Not much, because it was right when I left it the day before. I don't quantify the changes I make, but if on re-reading I think of something better to include, it goes in."

As he writes, he edits *each sentence*. "Yes, it's crazy, it can be a pain and stops the flow, but it's how I've always done it and after more than forty books I can't see myself changing. I'm stopping after every sentence. I suppose the danger is that if I don't have a clear idea what I'm trying to write, I can be so close to the text that I forget what's gone before or still to come. But I'm a planner. At the start of my career I'd write a chapter-by-chapter synopsis. These days it's mostly in my head and I'll have spent several weeks in the planning and made notes before I start. There aren't many mistakes but it's no good being smug about it. No one is all-knowing and the copyeditor will find things."

Peter finds it useful to read dialogue out loud. "There's a real danger with my navel-gazing method that the dialogue will come out in the same kind of deathless prose I'm aiming for in the rest of the book. I have to remind myself people don't speak the way I write. By speaking the dialogue aloud I can hear the voices. People don't often talk for long in a grammatical way. You have to reflect this, curb your tendency to write correctly."

Later when the proofs are sent to him for checking he looks for "Spelling errors that have crept in and the odd punctuation mark. It's fatal to get too involved in the story, or you miss things you're supposed to be looking for. And every error risks a break in the reader's concentration."

Every error risks a break in the reader's concentration.

Make yourself read this out loud every time you can't be bothered editing.

Sheila O'Flanagan – Editing a third of a book at a time

Best-selling Irish author Sheila O'Flanagan says, "For me, there are two kinds of editing. One is creative – which deals with the development of the plot and characters. The other is technical, which involves grammatical editing and looking at the structure of individual paragraphs and sentences prior to any comments made by a copyeditor.

"I do a substantial amount of both rewriting and creative editing as I work. Generally I tend to look at the novel in approximate thirds. I work on the first third, doing a lot of rewriting as I go. Then as I progress, I continually move back and forward between new material and the material I've already written and reworked, making editorial enhancements all the time. This means as I'm working on the second third of the novel, I've hopefully a limited amount of editing left to do to the first third, and so on. Obviously when I've reached the end, I look at the entire work as objectively as possible. At this point I'll have done the majority of the rewriting and most of the creative editing will be relatively straightforward. Then I move on to the technical side, working on the structure of the language. I also check for the overuse of certain words and phrases.

"It generally takes me nine months to get the book written and edited, plus additional time for reviewing any issues raised by the copyeditor afterwards. Sometimes these are very minor but sometimes copyeditors can raise questions that affect timelines within the plot. No matter how much editing you do, there's always something!"

Monica McInerney – Read, print, edit

Different editing methods work for best-selling Irish novelist Monica McInerney.

"Once the first draft is written, I print it out in full and read it in one sitting. I never read it in my office. I usually read it in bed, so it feels as though I'm reading a finished book, not my work-in-progress. I make copious notes, then return to the computer the next day and begin to make all the changes. I then print and read and edit again. I probably do that three or four times, then pass it to two trusted people to read – my sister and my husband, who have been my first readers for all ten of my novels. I take in their thoughts and comments, make more changes, print again, read again, edit again.

"After that, usually right on my deadline, I email it to my publishers in Australia, the UK and the USA. After a week or so, I receive their three, often different sets of editorial notes. I spend the following weeks mulling over their suggestions, making more changes, once again going through the print, read, edit process. I probably read my own novel thirty or more times before it's finally as good as I can make it. That official editing process, from sending the manuscript to my publishers to my final proof read of the typeset pages prior to the book going to the printers, usually takes three to four months."

Tim Bowler – First get it written, then get it right

Multi-award-winning author Tim Bowler says, "My approach is first get it written, then get it right. I write the first draft without any particular thought of beauty or style and focus simply on getting the ideas down. If that first draft is rubbish, which it often is, I might throw the whole thing away and do another rough draft or three or however many, again focusing on the matter of the story rather than the manner of the telling. I keep putting down words until I've got the rough-hewn story in place, until I've got it written. Then I concentrate on getting it right and this part might loosely be referred to as editing.

"Editing covers a multitude of activities – cutting, adding, changing, tweaking, rewriting, revising (which literally means re-seeing), and most of all – in the final stages – honing the words until the text is as good as I can make it. The process of writing has become less messy than it used to be before computers came along. In the days when I wrote longhand or on typewriters, I was literally rewriting complete drafts of books. I quite often threw away chunks of fifty or sixty thousand words – I once threw away eighty-five thousand – and started again.

"Computers have made life much easier from the editing

point of view. I'm not referring here to spellcheck and computer-generated grammar checks and editing tools. Apart from spellcheck, I don't use such things. I'm talking about the ability to amend text as you go without having to do the extensive rewriting that used to be necessary. It's made my own approach to writing much easier. I can produce my rough-hewn early drafts just as I used to but tidying them a little as I go along. Normally I don't have to write an entirely new draft of something now. I can cut and paste things as I go, add new stuff, take out rubbish, and push on through to the end of that rough version.

"My approach to each writing session when composing a raw draft is to read over the passage I last wrote, perhaps do a gentle tidy, get my head back in the current of the story, then push on. I don't worry if something isn't well written at this stage because I know I'll be coming back later to sort that out. I drive on through to the end of the draft and, when I have that, I go to town on the editing. I try to stand back and see the story as a whole. Does it work? What's good? What's bad? Is this character believable? Is that scene convincing? Would that person really act in such a way? Is that passage overwritten? Understanding these things is, for me, a wholly instinctive process. I don't have any kind of checklist. I just go over the manuscript again and again until I feel I've knocked it into some kind of readable shape. Then I get feedback from my wife, my editor, and my agent. After pondering what they've said, I go back to the manuscript and work on until I feel I've got it right."

Sarah Duncan – Editing in scenes

Romance author Sarah Duncan edits in scenes. "I rewrite and rewrite and rewrite – 26 drafts in one case! There isn't an absolute distinction between each draft, just when I felt it was time to move on to a new document. I always look at the big picture first and get the novel into the right shape before I start doing detailed line editing, although some will come as part of the rewriting process. I work a lot with index cards, one card per scene, which means you can see the shape of a novel easily and work out what needs to be added or subtracted. About the last thing I do is put it into chapters.

"When I'm editing I look at it on a scene-by-scene basis checking it's doing what I want it to do – tell the story, develop emotions, build pictures of places. I add a lot of detail at this stage, usually either character thoughts or location description. I make sure each paragraph has one bit that I think has pizazz. It could be a great verb or an arresting image, or something emotionally charged. Or funny – it doesn't matter what. I've been known to highlight each special bit to ensure I've got enough throughout the text.

"How long depends on the book. Some are easy to write, some are much harder work."

Sue Moorcroft – Editing in layers

Novelist Sue Moorcroft works in drafts, editing in a layered fashion until she is happy.

"For a novel, I do multiple drafts and each draft has a purpose. This may vary from book to book but, loosely –

1. First draft gets the story down.
2. Then I revise, sorting out inconsistencies and cutting out the ugliest sentences and tightening the loosest writing, trying to see where my story works or doesn't, tying in loose ends.
3. Probably a draft to incorporate more research and to 'put the reader there' will follow.
4. And definitely one to concentrate on the tensions between hero and heroine – I write romantic fiction – and provide the sizzle I need.
5. Finally, I concentrate on the writing, culling my pet words such as *suddenly, abruptly, just*; weak qualifiers

such as *somewhat, very* and *rather*; passive sentences and empty phrases. I try and ensure that I've used colour and imagery. I hunt through my imagination for exactly the phrases that please me most.

6. Then my editor gets hold of the book and I get revision notes.

7. Sometimes there's a second round of revisions.

8. Then the copyedit and the line edit.

I appreciate that my novel-writing process may seem messy to some, but that's the way I work. I think of it as writing in layers."

Dani Collins – Editing at What Comes Next? moments

Canadian romance author Dani Collins wrote every day for 25 years before having her first novel accepted. This meant she's developed more confidence in her voice and style than the average new writer. A confidence that's essential now, as she works to tight deadlines and must edit quickly.

"I take as much time for editing as I can after finishing the book and before its deadline. My most recent first draft finished on Saturday night. I turned it in on the following Wednesday night, so spent approximately 18 hours editing. When the revision letter comes, I usually have 30 days to turn it around and typically finish within a week or so.

"Throughout the writing process I go back to page one probably six or eight times. Anytime I have a What Comes Next? moment I reread the pages I have and revise where necessary, often rewriting scenes at that point. So I have a fairly clean draft once I reach The End and don't typically have major rewrites in that last week. It's more about cleaning up the actual prose then, not so much about refining the story.

"I don't have a formal editing checklist. My first priority is serving the development of the romance. I often rewrite interactions with secondary characters so they're impacting the romance rather than taking over the story with stolen bracelets or what have you.

"I make a point of killing *just* as often as possible. It's one of my bad habits along with 'ly' words and using more than one adjective to describe something. Novelist friend Kay Gregory told me the best advice she ever received was to pick the one adjective that's doing the most work and keep it. Cut the other.

"I look closely at emotions. Readers come to romance for the emotional journey of falling in love. I want to be fresh and realistic. How a character reacts is also the best opportunity to develop character so I always look at a word like *angry* and try to drill past that to the reason they're angry. Are they feeling guilty? Defensive? What's really going on here?

"Working with an editor, there are a few stages of revision. There's a developmental edit where they might ask for scenes to be rewritten, then another revision letter that digs into more detailed changes and finally a line edit.

"Harlequin Mills & Boon editors offer general revision requests like, 'You've strayed away from the romance here and the sexual tension has fallen off.' They provide suggestions and I've either been able to adapt them into the story or they've given me a jumping off point for something I like better. Given that it's usually a month or so after submitting that I receive feedback, I go into revisions with fresh eyes and often tweak other things at that point."

Which method works for you?

As you can see, each writer evolves their own editing pattern based on personal writing habits and the needs of their editor or publisher.

Anything goes. It doesn't matter how you do it so long as the end product is a good read. One where errors don't get in the reader's way.

Your job is to find what works for you.

Exercise

Go to a book launch or author talk at your local library or bookshop. Ask the writer how they edit. Each writer is different. You'll often learn something new.

Short Story Writers
Explain Their Editing Techniques

If it feels wrong, fix it

I rely on instinct when it comes to editing my short stories. If it doesn't feel right, I have another look at the basic building blocks. Substantive editing, in other words. If I'm stumped but believe the story has potential, I ask writer friends to read it. There's nothing like a second pair of eyes.

For example, my friend Bruce Thomson offered the following comments on my story *Deadlines*:

"I have a problem with a bread-eating ghost. In my perhaps traditionalist view, ghosts shouldn't be able to eat or do anything which involves experiencing tactile pleasure. Perhaps he should only gaze longingly at the bread?

"I'd also consider cutting down the first bit and adding more suspense at the end. As an investigative reporter, maybe she could look into the case herself rather than her editor telling her everything?

"Finally I wonder if this is right for *Woman's Day*. Shouldn't there be a love interest?"

He was right about the ghost so I had him gaze longingly at the bread rather than actually eating it. But romance didn't feel right for this story. That helped me see it wasn't really a *Woman's Day* story. I added suspense and sold the story to *The Weekly News*.

Another story that fell at the first hurdle was *Expectations*. I knew there was a problem but couldn't see it. Writing friend Lynne Hackles opened my eyes:

"I was just thinking how good this story was and you hit me with a change of viewpoint. You can't go head-hopping even though I realise you want to get Helen's opinion across."

With one viewpoint throughout, the story sold to *Fiction Feast*.

Big picture changes can be the hardest ones to spot yourself. Yet they're crucial.

When in doubt, ask. If it feels wrong, it needs to be fixed.

That's my method.

Now let's ask other short story writers what they do.

John Floyd – A triage approach

"After my first draft, I go back through the story with sort of a triage approach, trying to address the worst problems first, then the less serious problems, and so on. For me, the most important things are clarity, structure, characters and conflict, so I attack those first. That done, I turn my attention to style issues – grammar, word choice, word usage, sentence construction, paragraph construction, capitalisation, spelling and punctuation. Then I get really nitpicking, watching for typos, extra spaces between words, apostrophes that are the wrong way and so on. As for a checklist, I don't have one written out, but I suppose I have one in my head."

Kate Willoughby – Fix and adjust until it feels done

"I don't have a checklist, nor do I edit in stages. I just read and reread and fix and adjust until it feels done. I revise during the writing process. However once I get to the end, I go back over the story several times. I don't stop until I feel the story is as good as I can get it. To me, editing and revising are the same thing. It's fixing mistakes, refining language, clarifying ideas. It's the time when you step back and look at the whole, at pacing, at characterisation. I'll fine tune the humour and cut out stuff that's not necessary. My revising process isn't organised. Some people do a characterisation pass, then a conflict pass... I just read the story, and when I notice something that doesn't seem right, I work on it until it DOES seem right."

Ginny Swart – Keeping a To Be Finished file

"Sometimes I write a story and send it off somewhere that same night. I usually regret this because later I think of things I could've changed. I know that old saying about putting it in your desk drawer for a week and then looking at it again, but I never learn!

"Other times I start a story, with maybe what I consider a brilliant opening line and three paragraphs on I can see it's going nowhere. So I banish it into my To Be Finished File and it can stay there for days or months. Even years. Every now and then I fish it out and read what's there and sometimes have an inspiration about the ending. Or sometimes I think of changes I need to make so it'll work better.

I've found in general that stories I fiddle about with are often disasters."

Teresa Ashby – Read it aloud

"I don't consciously have an editing checklist. But I make sure I've been consistent with spellings and don't change from, say, 'doctor' to 'dr' or from 'fifteen' to '15'. I also check the chapters by using the search facility in Word. I search for 'Chapter' then go through and make sure I haven't missed any numbers or have two chapter fours. I read it aloud because while your eye may not pick up a wrong or missing word, your ears will. It also helps with making sure dialogue flows. If you stumble over the words, something needs to change."

Della Galton – A checklist in my head

"Personally when it comes to short fiction I do the following:

1. Draft one – get it on paper. I finish a short story in its entirety before I do much editing. I write directly on to a computer so I edit out basic mistakes as I notice them. I prefer my first drafts to make sense.

2. Draft two – I go through and make sure the story actually works. Does it have a strong enough beginning, middle and end? Are the plot/characters believable? Is it suitable for its intended market?

3. Draft three – I do a more detailed check for things like repetition of words/sentences. I check continuity, for example make sure I haven't changed a character's name or eye colour half way through.

4. Draft four – I do the nitty gritty proof reading draft – check spelling, grammar, punctuation, missing words and layout.

"One important thing I also do is to leave a cooling off period of at least three days, between draft two and draft three. It's then much easier to edit your work and see repetition and obvious mistakes. I also recommend that if you do any substantial rewriting after you've proof read a piece, that you proofread again. Most mistakes in final drafts are the result of changes being made after the proof reading stage."

Exercise

Check out the websites and blogs of well-known short story writers. Read about their editing experiences and ask any questions you may have. In addition, writing magazines often provide an opportunity for readers to pose questions.

Editors Explain Their Editing Techniques – Deborah Halverson

I asked Deborah Halverson, veteran freelance editor and award-winning writer and founder of DearEditor.com how much editing she'd advise a first time novelist to do before approaching a professional editor. And should a writer approach an editor before seeking an agent?

A professional edit

Deborah: "Editors and agents receive hundreds of submissions each month yet only publish a dozen or so titles annually – many from authors they already know are professionally competitive and saleable. In the face of those odds, why wouldn't you submit the best work you're able to craft, employing a professional editor's level of craft expertise and market awareness?

"A pre-submission substantive editing is essential. The editor will assess the plot and character arcs to make sure everything builds logically, believably, and with increasing tension to the climactic event and the final maturity/triumph/wisdom you seek for that character. The editor won't tinker with sentences or words because those things will change as the writer reworks scenes, chapters, even whole plotlines.

"A second edit is advisable to make sure they've accomplished what they needed and haven't exposed other issues in the process. If you're new to this, it isn't likely one edit-and-revision will lead to the final draft. If it's not fiscally possible to do a second edit, it's not, but don't short-change your career solely for the sake of keeping costs low.

"About 60% of writers I work with come back for a second edit, letting me assess their success with the revision and point out where more work is needed.

"If a writer plans to self-publish, I strongly recommend they do that second edit and then a follow-up line edit. It costs you nothing to write the book and you can upload it to e-retailers at minimal expense, so many see the possibility to make money without spending any. Or they are confident in their ability to handle editing on their own or with critique groups.

"But many self-published works could have stronger Big Picture elements and voice and exhibit many typos or distracting language/punctuation quirks. The editor has the expertise to do that kind of work as well as the distance or fresh eye to spot the weaknesses."

My next question to Deborah was: *What basic mistakes or areas needing much improvement do you see in the novels sent to you for substantive editing?*

A slow opening

Deborah: "A common pitfall is the story starts in the wrong place, at the wrong time. Think of the character who wakes to an alarm to start her day, picks out her clothes and examines herself in the mirror so you can describe her looks and style, then has breakfast and passes her significant other in the kitchen – or notably does not – so you can hear what her plan is for the day and what she thinks about it and who's going to play a part.

"Too much story set-up slows the opening. Writers must be patient about delivering backstory facts, teasing them out as needed. Let the readers figure out some things. You don't need to explain Susie is Annie's best friend. Show them completing each other's sentences in a conversation.

"Strong openings present the character in a situation that shows her actively demonstrating her strengths, weaknesses, concerns, and goals. For example, a book could open by introducing a lady getting ready for work, dressing in a fine suit and then heading out. Or it could have her at her desk, answering important phone calls and explain how she got this job and how much time she spends there versus with her family.

"A better opening scene could have that character rummaging under a raised porch, belly-crawling through the dust and cobwebs despite wearing her pink designer business suit. The reader will be intrigued by this disparity, will start working out the personality of this character. Is there someone barking orders to her, showing her subservience and revealing her life or career circumstances? Is this all her idea, willingly sacrificing one thing for something she finds more important? What is she looking for and what does it mean to her – and what brought her to this moment in her life?

"This gives the reader something to work through. Don't start the story at the beginning of things, but rather in the middle and then patiently reveal how that character came to be there doing that thing and toward what end."

Common mistakes

Question: *The second stage of editing is fixing the general style – checking for continuity and consistency, choice of words, sentence construction. Does everything make sense? Could you give details of specific problems here?*

Deborah: "Sentence variety, or lack of it is a common issue – too many clauses, sentence after sentence after sentence. You need to work in declarative statements, too. And you don't always have to tell us what a character's doing as they're saying something.

"Here's an example. All but the first sentence start with a clause. It feels over-written.

John couldn't remember a time when the road didn't call to her. For all of her twelve years, the long hazy road through the desert had called to her and seemed to lead away from the pub, the only home she knew. Somehow the Last Chance Pub and Grill survived, clinging to its plot of sandy land that stretched in every direction of this *Grand Canyon State. Except for a few cars that passed in the night, this corner of Arizona seemed deserted. Looking at the wavy horizon, she dreamed of what it would be like to leave. Hearing her father, she turned and went downstairs."*

Question: *The third stage is the nuts and bolts – spelling, punctuation – copyediting. What mistakes do you commonly find?*

Deborah: "There's a lack of understanding of basic comma rules particularly in dialogue, with dialogue tags. Also non-speaking verbs are often used as speaking verbs. Some examples:

You cannot smile dialogue, as in this: *'That was seriously hilarious,' she smiled.*

You can't laugh it either, or frown it, or hiss lines that have no s's.

'I didn't want to go.' I said should be *'I didn't want to go,' I said.*

And *John grabbed the boy by his thin shoulder, 'Don't do it.'* should be *John grabbed the boy by his thin shoulders. 'Don't do it.'* or *John grabbed the boy by his thin shoulders, saying, 'Don't do it.'*

"Comma use with clauses is an issue, too.

"Another problem is rules of hyphenated adjectives not followed, such as *the funnel shaped generator* and *a handsome looking guy. Handsome-looking* is an adjective modifying the noun *guy.* Without that hyphen that dude is a handsome guy who is looking. We don't even need the word *looking* because handsome implies that."

Question: *Is it advisable for a writer to employ the same editor for each of these stages?*

"Trust is essential when it comes to evaluating editorial input and changing your baby. There's the risk that bringing in a new editor at subsequent changes will derail you if that editor calls out substantive changes. Some view that as beneficial while for others their confidence in the project takes a hit.

"In practice, I don't do much line editing as writers opt to handle that themselves. I refer to other trusted editors if a submission isn't scoring any hits with publishers or agents. Someone else might see what the author and I are now too close to see."

Question: *What are the essential editing tools for each stage?*

Deborah: "Writers must learn how to self-edit. Even if they're going to work with editors, they need to learn to spot their strengths, weakness, and mistakes. I have a self-editing handout in *Writing Fiction For Dummies* and a chapter that walks you through the process."

Editors Explain Their Editing Techniques – Rebecca LuElla Miller

I posed these same questions to Rebecca LuElla Miller, freelance writer and editor and author of *Power Elements of Story Structure*.

Question: *How much editing should a first time novelist do before approaching a professional editor? Should a writer approach an editor before seeking an agent?*

A professional edit

Rebecca: "Those hoping to publish traditionally who have a solid grasp of grammar, story structure, character development and so on, may never need a professional editor aside from the ones their publisher will provide.

"However many new novelists don't know what they don't know, and therefore won't realise they need a professional editor until they've received a collection of form rejections. My advice to first timers is to get involved in a good critique group and/or get a critique from an agent or editor.

"Critiques expose problem areas. If the problems are sizable, the novel may not be ready for a professional edit. A mentoring program, instruction books, or classes might give the writer what's needed most. Only after addressing the things the critique uncovered should a professional editor be hired. This approach may seem backwards, but if there are major structural problems, the writer will rewrite a good portion of the story and any line editing paid for will be lost.

"On the other hand, those who have a solid understanding of story elements and grammar who plan to self-publish their work should hire a professional editor as soon as they've polished their manuscript to the best of their ability."

Question: *What basic mistakes, or areas needing much improvement, do you see in the overall structure of novels sent to you for substantive editing?*

Story opening

Rebecca: "The number one problem is starting a story with a character who doesn't want or need anything and therefore has no plan of action. Instead, stuff happens and the character reacts.

"Here's one sample of what I said to a client regarding this problem: 'The opening pages of a novel should still introduce the reader to something the character wants or needs. In that way, when the inciting incident happens to disrupt normal, it's easy to see the character will have to either set a new goal or change plans to accomplish what they want. I don't see your character's goal, want, or need. The character seems stuck . . . without any plan to make the best of [A] or [B]. They are surviving but don't seem to have a plan about how to do that either. Consequently, I don't have any reason to cheer for them.'"

Common mistakes

Question: *The second stage of editing is fixing the general style – checking for continuity and consistency, choice of words, sentence construction. Does everything make sense? Could you give details of specific problems?*

Rebecca: "Word choice, sentence construction, consistency and the rest vary widely. One person might fall in love with a certain sentence construction and not use enough variety, while another slips into the passive voice. One writer might have a problem with frequently repeating a word. One client relied on the word *turned* – every character was turning his head or turning to look or turning the doorknob. Another might misuse words. Problems in these areas are many. No novelist has them all, and none has precisely the same ones as everyone else."

Question: *The third stage is the nuts and bolts – spelling, punctuation – copyediting. What mistakes do you commonly find?*

Rebecca: "Without a doubt, commas rule in the area of mechanical errors. Since most publishing houses in the USA prefer *Chicago Manual of Style* for fiction, that's the one I rely on.

"Italics are also problematic because new writers want to use them for internal discourse. Such usage was once common but more and more publishers are aligning their internal guidelines to the industry norm, which states internal discourse should be put inside quotation marks or left unmarked."

Question: *Is it advisable for a writer to employ the same editor for each of these stages?*

Rebecca: "Publishers traditionally use up to four editors/proof-readers. Few writers can afford such luxury. The best approach is to hire an editor to cover stage one issues. After revising, the writer can hire an editor, either the same or different, for the next three stages. If money isn't an issue, a third proofreading pass is advisable. A fresh set of eyes helps at this stage."

Question: *What are the essential editing tools for each stage?*

Rebecca: "For the first stage, the editor needs extensive knowledge of story structure, development of character and point of view. The editor's job is not to dictate fixes but to suggest by way of illustration.

"In the second stage, the editor needs understanding of story-telling devices. It requires mastery of dialogue techniques and description that moves the story forward rather than stalling the action.

"The final stage requires an editor who knows the nuances of fiction writing as opposed to nonfiction. An example is pronoun reference. When I started, I slavishly corrected pronouns to nouns if they weren't in close proximity to their antecedent – the noun they renamed or replaced. In fiction, the result can be needless repetition. A character rarely thinks of himself using his own name. Clarity should govern a strict adherence to grammar rules. If a personal pronoun is separated from its antecedent, but readers still know to whom it refers, it doesn't need to be changed."

Rebecca recommends Noah Lukeman's *The First Five Pages* (ISBN: 978-0684857435)

Exercise

Check out the blogs and websites of freelance editors. Editing problems and experiences are often discussed.

Example:
Lowcountry Bribe By Hope Clark

How Hope edits

Hope Clark is author of the award-winning Carolina Slade Mystery Series. Here she describes her editing process:

"1. Finish the rough draft on screen.
2. Let it sit for a week or two.
3. Edit on screen for the big picture aspects. Does it have a beginning, middle and ending? Does it open strong and end strong, making the point clear? Did the middle sag? Is the plot solid?
4. Edit on screen for flow, syntax, and flavour. Tweak dialogue. Revisit the climax. Dissect the pivotal scenes. Make the setting three-dimensional and the characters real.
5. Edit on screen for grammar, typos and spelling.
6. Print out and pull out your red pen. Read with a hard editor's eye, slowly and methodically. You'll see the story differently on paper than you did on the screen.
7. Now, read it aloud. You can read it to someone or they can read it to you. If the other person is not a serious writer, have them read it to you, so your ear can catch the mistakes, lulls and boredom.
8. Have a beta reader who is a writer read it.
9. Have a beta reader who is a voracious reader read it. Don't waste your time with someone who's not a solid, well-read recreational reader. They won't catch the boo-boos.
10. Hire an editor.
11. Find a copyeditor.
12. Find a proofreader."

From draft to publication – *Lowcountry Bribe*

Question: *In* Lowcountry Bribe, *where you changed who killed who – can you explain WHY you made such a drastic change? And how you came to change it FOUR times?*

Hope: "When writing a book, you have to make changes as your thought processes grow. You'll write a book in a given direction, read it, then realise it's not what you'd hoped for, or you come up with something even better in the journey. Or if your beta readers have a problem, or your editor has a better idea, you have to learn to go with the flow.

"In *Lowcountry Bribe* (spoiler alert), in the first version Wayne (the federal agent) showed up and saved the day. He killed Jesse (the antagonist). It was just Wayne, Jesse and the protagonist Carolina Slade. But it felt too obvious, plus this was Slade's book, not Wayne's. So I changed it so that Wayne showed up to save the day and was injured and incapacitated. Slade had to save the day. My critique group said it was okay not earth shattering.

"So I re-analysed the What If of the scene. What if Wayne didn't even know where she was? I perked up and rewrote. Slade was kidnapped and Wayne was on his way to meet her. He has no idea where she is. Cops everywhere are hunting for her. But she realises she's on her own.

"Then, in editing earlier chapters, I sought something to make Jesse a deeper character. Make him likeable as a bad guy, with more dimension. So I gave him a brother with a slight mental disability. Jesse keeps peppermints in his pocket to give Ren when the little brother gets upset. Since Ren is like a shadow to Jesse, I carried Ren throughout the book into the final scene. Now there's Jesse, Ren and Slade in the scene where all heck hits the fan. Slade kills Jesse accidentally, leaving her with Ren who's totally unpredictable, and suddenly Slade is in another threatening situation with just Ren. Added a phenomenal depth to the ending.

"You never get that depth in the first writing, I don't care who you are as a writer. That's why you remain ever open to change, and why you need other readers who are savvy, not just relatives who like your work."

Question: *When the publisher asked you to change it again – did you agree with their change? Did it feel right? Did they choose one of your previous murderers?*

Hope: "The publisher changed how Jesse was murdered, the gymnastics in the room, and yes, it did feel right. I'd already decided the heroine had to do the killing, but the weapon and conversation and movement in the room was altered a lot. Too many writers think publishers and editors don't get it when it's actually the other way around. When you bring in an editor and publisher, you're also bringing in new ideas. They want you to be successful and they have more experience than you do in what sells in the marketplace. Listen to them. You don't have to follow them like a puppy dog but you do need to attempt to infuse their ideas in your work. I go back and forth with my editor but we usually convince each other of our best suggestions. When I hear an author digging in, saying they understand their book better than some editor or publisher, I see an author who's limiting their future."

Question: *Could you explain why you decided to write out a character? How much reworking did this involve?*

Hope: "To avoid an office of all women, I'd written in a male assistant to Carolina Slade. He was reliable when she distrusted all the women at one point. However, a savvy member of my critique group pointed out he added nothing to the advancement of the story. It was just a feel-good, two-dimensional character for her to lean on, when I needed to ratchet up the tension, not give

Slade a comfy reprieve in this character. Here is where I learned that every single character has to advance the story, no matter how small or secondary. So I got rid of him. It required reworking at least six or seven chapters.

"I don't know why people fuss at reworking chapters. It's like refusing to use more colour in a painting because it means cleaning your brush, pulling out another tube of paint, and taking more time to work it yet again. Yes, it's more time and work, but why wouldn't you want to do it if it makes the story better?"

Question: *Could you explain why you decided to add a new character? What did this involve?*

Hope: "I explained adding Jesse's brother Ren. He's a small player (you think), but he perpetually advances the story and adds depth to Jesse. However, when the manuscript was in the publisher's hands, the editor (who was from the city) didn't understand why Slade didn't call the cops more often when bad things happened. There were two places where she felt Slade was stupid not to call the cops. So, I rewound the story yet again and created a likeable cop. He had a job to do, and Slade was distrusting of cops by halfway through the book but Deputy Donald reminded her some cops were good and the insertion of Donald in the story removed any sense of doubt about the reality of Slade's actions/inactions. The publisher was happy yet the character didn't deter Slade's mission. Again, more depth to the story.

"Writers rush to publish because they've learned a backlist garners attention. Readers like an author and immediately want more of their books. So a relatively new author, especially self-published, fights hard to crank out books, usually too fast. The stories might even be respectable reads but I know those books could be better in ways they can't fathom in the rush of seeing them in print."

Part IV

When is Editing Finished?

When is Editing Finished?

Finding the happy medium

Editing a story or novel isn't like painting a house. You don't necessarily realise when the job's finished. There's no clear cut-off point. We each have to make the decision that our manuscript is as good as we can make it.

Many writers unintentionally send work out that contains typos, errors in punctuation and grammar, and even larger problems such as superfluous characters, confused point of view and inadequate plot development.

It's easy to stop before the editing job is properly done. We see evidence of it every time we open a magazine or newspaper.

But what about the other end of the spectrum? Is it possible to go too far? Continue editing beyond what the story needs? Can the life be strangled out of prose?

We've all read stories that have lost their sparkle.

How do you find the happy medium?

How do we know when editing is finished?

For me it's when I can no longer stand the sight of a story. Or when I'm able to read through a printed version without changing anything. Better still, when I can read it out loud without my audience walking away.

Let's ask some other writers how they know editing is finished.

Viewpoints

Sheila O'Flanagan

"For most authors, editing is never really finished. If I read back over anything I've written, even years later, I find something I want to change. But you have to arrive at a point when the time you're spending on every word isn't justified by the affect it's having on your work. It's hard to do. For me, it's when my editor at the publishing house has read the copy I've sent and has no more comments. At that point I realise it's the best it can possibly be – at that moment in time. And I have to let it go."

Hope Clark

"In my opinion you cannot edit too much unless you have no idea what you're writing. If you have purpose in your project and understand the direction of your story then you'll know when the editing's done. How many times do you edit a story? Wrong question. The question is more along the lines of how many ways can you edit. If you wonder about whether you're editing enough, chances are you aren't."

Monica McInerney

"It never stops. Even now, if I pick up a printed copy of one of my earlier books, I'll find a sentence I wish I could change."

Teresa Ashby

"I've spent a whole weekend editing and it's amazing how many typos I can miss – and my husband can miss – after several reads and then when I sent myself a copy of the final draft to my kindle, more mistakes leap out.

"I've never regretted cutting words even when it's been something I was really happy with – once it's gone and you see how much better it is, you soon lose any regret!"

Lynne Hackles

"I often tell students that editing has to stop sometime and if Shakespeare came back he'd start editing his work again. No one, except a fool, can ever be 100% satisfied."

Della Galton

"I think it depends on the way you write and possibly also on what type of writing you do as both these things will affect the quality of your first draft. I know writers whose first draft is little more than notes. Their second draft might be to turn their notes into a piece of readable prose with a structure and their third to polish. How many drafts you need to do depends on how finished your first draft is – which may also depend on the speed you write it. Perhaps the kind of editing you do is more important than the amount of times you do it."

Sarah Duncan

"You've done enough rewriting/editing when you've done all you can possibly and have no niggling questions or doubts. There's no point sending it out if you think there might be something lacking. People aren't stupid. If you think there's something lacking they will too, although irritatingly it's not always the same thing. You have to believe it's the very very best you can do with no ifs or buts or maybes."

Jane Wenham-Jones

"It's finished when you're cross-eyed and seeing double! Seriously, you stop when you really feel you can't do any more. And if you've got to the point where you're deleting words, then putting them back in again and then wondering whether to remove them after all, you've reached that point. You'll still find typos later. But fortunately in the production of a book, there are lots of stages at which you can tweak further and there'll also be input from other people. One needs to put distance between oneself and the finished work so I'd say when you feel you've done your utmost, send it off to the agent, editor, publisher or whoever and see what they turn up.

"If you're talking the very last time you see this work before it's printed, then all you can do is trust your instincts and possibly ask someone else to take a look.

The important thing is to never say, 'That'll do.' Because

unless it is the very, very best you can make it, it won't!"

Simon Whaley

"When is editing finished? I think that depends on the project. With short stories, ensure you've got your point across clearly, and checked spelling and punctuation so everything's coherent. There's little point in titivating for days on end because if it's accepted, magazine editors sometimes rewrite openings and endings. And some short story editors have changed character names too, so you don't have so much control over the finished published piece.

"Larger projects, such as novels are more personal and it's worth spending time getting them right. But if you get to the stage that Oscar Wilde did, of spending all morning taking a comma out and then all afternoon putting it back in again, it's time to move on."

Dani Collins

"Editing is clarifying and refining. Learning to stop editing when you've got the right balance of brevity and clarity is a skill you develop with practice. Editing should always strengthen the piece. Once it begins to take away, it's time to stop."

Tim Bowler

"There comes a point where you have to stand back and say the story's finished. The honing could always go on longer. There's always something that could possibly be better if you just squeezed a little more juice out of it. But the story has to live and breathe and have its say and it won't do that if you refuse to let it go. Even some of the greatest stories in history could probably have been better if their authors had worked them a little longer but, if they'd done that, we might not have those masterpieces at all. For me, editing is the part of the process that takes most time. Writing the raw drafts can be quick but editing is always slow.

But there comes a point when you've cut and changed and fiddled and rewritten and honed and honed, when something inside you goes click. It's a click that says let the story go now. It's ready. So I let it go. And hope."

Conclusion

The experts tell us 90% of writing consists of rewriting. A first draft is just the beginning.

Whether it's a novel or short story doesn't matter. Editing is not optional, and there are no shortcuts. Editing will transform your first draft into the best piece you can write.

Show your work the respect it deserves. Put it away, then rework it until it gleams.

Never send out your first draft.

Don't time yourself. Don't count how many times you go through, trying to improve your work. What does it matter if it takes 20 reads before you get it right? Or 50 reads?

Respect yourself – and respect your reader. Make it as good as you possibly can.

There's no one-size-fits-all approach. The writers I interviewed for this book range from relative newcomers to household names. Each has evolved their own editing technique. You need to learn from their experience and find what works for you.

Part of being a published writer is simply realising that the first draft is just that. The real work now needs to begin.

In the ultra competitive world of publishing only the best will succeed. Modern readers are less forgiving than their predecessors. Everyone leads busy lives. If they're not gripped by your characters and care what happens, they'll move on to another author.

Edit is a four-letter word. It means hard work. Time. Pain.

But it's the only path to other four-letter words. Book deal. Sale. Cash. Fame.

So get on with it!

**COMPASS
BOOKS**

Compass Books focuses on practical and informative 'how-to' books for writers. Written by experienced authors who also have extensive experience of tutoring at the most popular creative writing workshops, the books offer an insight into the more specialised niches of the publishing game.